A VERY SHORT, FAIRLY INTERESTING AND REASONABLY CHEAP BOOK ABOUT

MANAGEMENT THEORY

[ALSO IN THIS SERIES]

A VERY SHORT,
FAIRLY INTERESTING AND
REASONABLY CHEAP BOOK ABOUT

GLOBALIZATION

LEO McCANN

SECOND EDITION

A VERY SHORT,
FAIRLY INTERESTING AND
REASONABLY CHEAP BOOK ABOUT

INTERNATIONAL BUSINESS

GEORGE CAIRNS AND
MARTYNA SLIWA

A VERY SHORT,
FAIRLY INTERESTING AND
REASONABLY CHEAP BOOK ABOUT

EMPLOYMENT RELATIONS

TONY DUNDON,
NIALL CULLINANE AND
ADRIAN WILKINSON

A VERY SHORT,
FAIRLY INTERESTING AND
REASONABLY CHEAP BOOK ABOUT

HUMAN RESOURCE MANAGEMENT

IRENA GRUGULIS

FOURTH EDITION

A VERY SHORT,
FAIRLY INTERESTING AND
REASONABLY CHEAP BOOK ABOUT

STUDYING ORGANIZATIONS

CHRIS GREY

A VERY SHORT,
A FAIRLY INTERESTING AND
REASONABLY CHEAP BOOK ABOUT
KNOWLEDGE MANAGEMENT

JOANNE ROBERTS

A VERY SHORT,
FAIRLY INTERESTING AND
REASONABLY CHEAP BOOK ABOUT

INTERNATIONAL MARKETING

AMANDA EARLEY

A VERY SHORT,
FAIRLY INTERESTING AND
REASONABLY CHEAP BOOK ABOUT
MANAGEMENT RESEARCH

EMMA BELL AND RICHARD THORPE

A VERY SHORT,
FAIRLY INTERESTING AND
REASONABLY CHEAP BOOK ABOUT
QUALITATIVE RESEARCH

SECOND EDITION

DAVID SILVERMAN

A VERY SHORT,
FAIRLY INTERESTING AND
REASONABLY CHEAP BOOK ABOUT
COACHING AND MENTORING

BOB GARVEY

A VERY SHORT,
FAIRLY INTERESTING AND
REASONABLY CHEAP BOOK ABOUT
STUDYING STRATEGY

SECOND EDITION

CHRIS CARTER, STEWART R. CLEGG
AND MARTIN KORNBERGER

THIRD EDITION

A VERY SHORT,
FAIRLY INTERESTING AND
REASONABLY CHEAP BOOK ABOUT

STUDYING LEADERSHIP

BRAD JACKSON AND KEN PARRY

A VERY SHORT, FAIRLY INTERESTING AND REASONABLY CHEAP BOOK ABOUT

MANAGEMENT THEORY

TODD BRIDGMAN
STEPHEN CUMMINGS

Los Angeles | London | New Delhi
Singapore | Washington DC | Melbourne

Los Angeles | London | New Delhi
Singapore | Washington DC | Melbourne

SAGE Publications Ltd
1 Oliver's Yard
55 City Road
London EC1Y 1SP

SAGE Publications Inc.
2455 Teller Road
Thousand Oaks, California 91320

SAGE Publications India Pvt Ltd
B 1/I 1 Mohan Cooperative Industrial Area
Mathura Road
New Delhi 110 044

SAGE Publications Asia-Pacific Pte Ltd
3 Church Street
#10-04 Samsung Hub
Singapore 049483

Editor: Ruth Stitt
Assistant editor: Jessica Moran
Production editor: Manmeet Kaur Tura
Copyeditor: Sarah Bury
Proofreader: Clare Weaver
Indexer: Cathryn Pritchard
Marketing manager: Lucia Sweet
Cover design: Wendy Scott
Typeset by: Cenveo Publisher Services
Printed in the UK

Library of Congress Control Number: 2020937087

British Library Cataloguing in Publication data

A catalogue record for this book is available from the
British Library

ISBN 978-1-5264-9514-3
ISBN 978-1-5264-9513-6 (pbk)

Contents

List of Figures and Tables

Figures

Table

About the Authors

Todd Bridgman is an Associate Professor in the School of Management at Victoria University of Wellington, New Zealand. Todd completed his PhD in organization studies at the University of Cambridge. His research interests lie at the intersection of management history, management education and critical management studies. In particular, he is interested in challenging conventional histories of management that appear in textbooks and writing alternative histories as a way of rethinking how management is taught to students. Todd edited *The Oxford Handbook of Critical Management Studies* (Oxford University Press, 2009) with Mats Alvesson and Hugh Willmott and his research won Best Paper prizes in *Human Relations* (with Stephen Cummings and Kenneth Brown) and *Academy of Management Learning & Education* (with Stephen Cummings, Colm McLaughlin and John Ballard). Todd is Co-Editor-in-Chief of the international journal *Management Learning* and is a member of the editorial boards of *Academy of Management Learning & Education* and *Organization*.

Stephen Cummings is Professor of Strategy and Innovation and Co-Director of The Atom Innovation Space, at Victoria University of Wellington. He completed his PhD at Warwick Business School. Stephen's research investigates how assumptions about history can limit innovation and he is currently Co-Chair of the Critical Management Studies Division at The Academy of Management. His recent books include *Handbook of Management and Creativity* (Edward Elgar, 2014 – with Chris Bilton), *Strategy Builder* (Wiley, 2015 – with Duncan Angwin), *A New History of Management* (Cambridge University Press, 2017 – with Todd Bridgman, John Hassard and Michael Rowlinson), and the forthcoming *The Past, Present and Future of Sustainable Management* (Palgrave – with Todd Bridgman). His article, 'Unfreezing Change as Three Steps', published in *Human Relations* (with Todd Bridgman and Kenneth Brown), has been downloaded over 250,000 times.

Acknowledgements

We owe special thanks to Chris Grey (Royal Holloway) for being an inspiring supervisor and mentor, and also for writing the book that spawned this book series. Thanks also to Alexandra Bristow (Open University) for sharing our belief that this was a book that needed to be written.

We would also like to acknowledge the support and encouragement we have received from colleagues over the years, whose work has informed the approach we develop in this book. In particular, Hugh Willmott (Cass Business School), Gibson Burrell (Lancaster University), Raza Mir (William Paterson University), Mark Learmonth (Durham University), Chris Bilton (University of Warwick), Bill Foster (University of Alberta), Christine Quinn Trank (Vanderbilt University), Gabie Durepos (Mount Saint Vincent University), Albert Mills (Saint Mary's University), Bill Cooke (University of York), Trish Genoe McLaren (Wilfrid Laurier University), Haridimos Tsoukas (University of Cyprus), Leon Prieto (Clayton State University), Simone Phipps (Middle Georgia State University), JC Spender (Fordham University), Ellen O'Connor (Dominican University), Scott Taylor (University of Birmingham), Emma Bell (Open University), John Roberts (University of Sydney) and Edward Wray-Bliss (Macquarie University).

This book draws on research we have done with valued colleagues, including John Hassard (University of Manchester), Michael Rowlinson (University of Exeter), Kenneth Brown (University of Iowa), John Ballard (Mount St. Joseph University), Colm McLaughlin (University College Dublin), Richard Badham (Macquarie University), Rebecca Bednarek (Victoria University of Wellington), and Oliver Pol (Victoria University of Wellington). This research would not have been possible without the help and guidance from library and archive staff at The Stevens Institute, Brandeis University, Harvard University, The Tavistock Institute, and University of Akron.

We are also grateful to colleagues who read and commented on parts of the manuscript: Ben Walker (Victoria University of Wellington), Colm McLaughlin (University College Dublin), Kira Lussier (University of Toronto) and Mark Hughes (University of Brighton). In addition, we received many useful suggestions on the proposal and draft chapters from anonymous reviewers via SAGE.

The entire draft was read and reviewed by management student Zoé Fuller. Zoé provided insightful comments and encouraged us to write in a style appropriate for our audience.

Finally, we appreciate the support we have received from SAGE throughout the project, especially from series editor Ruth Stitt, who commissioned the book and provided comments on draft chapters, from assistant editors Martha Cunneen and Jessica Moran, and from production editor Manmeet Kaur Tura.

Should You Buy This book?

This book is primarily aimed at university students who have studied an introduction to management course and wish to look further at the field's foundational theories. It is also for anyone who has encountered popular management ideas in their workplace and is curious to learn more about their origins.

You should buy this book if:

- You want to learn more about management theories that influence your experience of work
- You're interested in discovering myths surrounding management's most popular theories. For example, Maslow's famous pyramid of human needs was not created by Maslow, so who created it, and why?
- You're curious as to why the origins of management theories are often quite different from what is said about them in management textbooks
- You're looking for new and innovative ways of thinking about management, which comes from looking at management's theories critically

If you do read this book, we'd like to hear your feedback. Email us at todd.bridgman@vuw.ac.nz and stephen.cummings@vuw.ac.nz

1

Why Another Book on Management Theory?

If you've ever studied management (or even if you haven't) you've probably heard of its founders and their theories – Adam Smith (the division of labour), Max Weber (bureaucracy) and Frederick Taylor (scientific management). In a management course these would be covered early on, usually as part of Chapter 2 in the textbook which lays out a brief history of the field. You would then have covered topics such as motivation, group dynamics, and organizational culture. Here, too, you would have encountered theorists whose ideas formed the foundations of those fields, such as Abraham Maslow (motivation), Kurt Lewin (group dynamics) and Ed Schein (culture). This book is about these and other foundational theories of management. By 'management theory' we mean ideas that are intended to explain and inform management practice. Theory can be expressed in the form of concepts, models, frameworks or general principles.

You might be asking why, if these theories already get extensive coverage in management textbooks, do we need this book? In this introductory chapter we answer that question, explain why we wrote the book, why we think you should read it, and provide a brief overview of the chapters to follow.

A view widely held by university lecturers is that students are not really interested in management theory, especially theories from the distant past. If you scan any management textbook, you will see that the theories they include are mostly decades old, developed when the world was very different. You might have heard the view that we're living in a 'VUCA' world characterized by Volatility, Uncertainty, Complexity and Ambiguity, where change is happening at a rate faster than ever before. In a VUCA world, knowledge becomes obsolete in ever-shortening timeframes. Why, then, would we want to continue to teach theories that you apparently aren't interested in and have little or no contemporary relevance?

We've taught management courses to tens of thousands of undergraduate and postgraduate students and know that students *are* interested in foundational management theories – particularly once they can see how understanding these origins can help them. A historical appreciation of management theory can help you think more critically about why certain ideas are so popular, why they may not work, and what the alternatives might be. Explaining the value of a historical appreciation of management's development is the task we set ourselves for the remainder of this chapter and, indeed, the book as a whole. It is a task that involves challenging some fairly widely held assumptions about management theories. These include assumptions that theories quickly become obsolete, that today's theories are fundamentally different and better than those from the past, and that the main reason for learning management theory is to become a better manager.

In challenging these views, we not only argue that management theories from the past remain relevant today, but that understanding the origins of these theories is more important than ever. We also argue that the way these theories are presented in management textbooks and taught to students prevents us from realizing their full learning potential. Sadly, many textbooks present a distorted view of the founders' original ideas. As we explore later in this chapter, this can partly be attributed to the need for textbooks to condense theories into a simplified form that students can understand. However, we also believe there are ideological forces at play in management studies that obscure the original intent of theorists (many of whom were not theorists of management). Their theories are repackaged in a form that can be part of a manager's 'took-kit' – in other words, that can be used by managers in an attempt to improve the efficiency and productivity of their employees and to enhance the performance and profitability of their organizations. And through that process, the theory gets distorted and misunderstood.

Understanding how and why these misrepresentations happen gives us valuable insight into how management as a field of study has developed. It also creates a space for alternative ways of thinking about management to take hold. Given the pressing environmental, social and economic challenges the world faces today, it is a timely to think more creatively about people, organizations and how we work.

The enduring relevance of foundational theories in management

I would like to believe that various kinds of experiences and decades of academic research would expand our knowledge base. So it is sometimes a bit of a shock to see how much we thought we already knew 50 years ago and how little our conclusions have changed.

Ed Schein (2015a: 7–8)

Ed Schein has made an enormous contribution to the field of management studies for more than half a century. You might be familiar with his model of organizational culture with its three levels: artefacts, espoused values and basic assumptions (we will discuss it further in Chapter 4). He has also been influential in popularizing other well-known management theories, such as Lewin's unfreeze-change-refreeze model of organizational change (covered in Chapter 5). We can't think of a person better placed to assess the current state of management theory than Schein. As can be seen from the quotation above, Schein does not think there's been as much progress over the last 50 years as many believe.

There is no doubt that the quantity of management research being produced is increasing every year. In most universities, the business school is important because of the high demand for business qualifications, and management is often one of the largest subjects within those schools. Most management lecturers are required to produce research. The pressures to publish have intensified in recent years because of funding and prestige that accrues to those universities that perform highly in research.

But it is also the case that most of this research has very little impact. Faculty are rewarded for publishing in highly-ranked academic journals and many of these are behind publisher paywalls. Calls are growing louder for research to be made freely available, but even when research is open access, the readership of these articles remains small. Schein argues that management research has splintered into sub-fields that have their own jargon and therefore exclude all but a small number of academic insiders. Even if students, employees and managers can make sense of the academic jargon, they are likely to find the research sets out only to fill some small gap in the discipline's knowledge base.

Schein is not the only person concerned about a decline in substantially new theories about management (Alvesson and Sandberg, 2012). We have talked to textbook authors who say it is desperately difficult to find new theories to include – or at least new ideas that offer more than foundational ones. Like Schein, we believe that the growth of management research has in fact obscured rather than superseded the insights generated by the field's founders. Consequently, there is much still to be gained in better understanding those foundations.

There is another problematic aspect regarding the lack of relevance of management research. In the absence of new theories generated by academics, others, especially management consultants, have sought to fill the void with theories of their own. Schein notes that these ideas, often generated by surveys and presented in the form of frameworks, have little connection to the research produced by academics. These theories are products of what Drezner (2017) calls the 'ideas industry' and are often enthusiastically promoted by 'thought leaders' in TED talks and on social media (Bell et al., 2019). Thought leaders 'develop their own singular lens to explain the world, and then proselytize that worldview to anyone within earshot' (Drezner, 2017: 9). This is problematic because thought leaders are not like the traditional public intellectuals who encouraged people to question and challenge prevailing ideas in society. Thought leaders, says Drezner, are 'intellectual evangelists' who want us to accept their ideas uncritically and unconditionally. They demand true believers.

We think it is important for us all to be sceptical of claims made by thought leaders. While the promoters of popular management ideas always make claims to novelty, are they genuinely new ideas or recycled and repacked ideas from the past? The cyclical nature of management ideas has parallels with the fashion process, with ideas becoming popular before eventually fading and being replaced by more 'cutting-edge' ideas, only to re-emerge in some altered form in the future (Huczynski, 2006). Look at photos of what your parents wore when they were your age or listen to the music they liked then. You will see some differences, but (perhaps surprisingly, or painfully) you'll see and hear similarities as well. If we have no knowledge about the history of management theories, we cannot make accurate judgements about the claims of novelty made by thought leaders.

So, we argue that studying the origins of management theories helps us to be critical thinkers – a valuable skill to develop, particularly as a student. A principal aim of universities is to cultivate intellectual independence – to be exposed to a wide range of perspectives, to use these perspectives to generate different ways of understanding the world, to think critically about the strengths and limitations of all perspectives and, ultimately, to form our own judgements.

While we're on the subject of thinking critically about popular ideas, let's return to the claim that in today's VUCA world the pace of change, especially technological change, such as artificial intelligence, is unprecedented. Remember, this argument is put forward as a reason why we need not learn management theories from the past. Is the world really changing faster than before? There is certainly very troubling evidence that the Earth's climate is experiencing rapid change, but what about changes in the business world? To answer that question, we need to understand the past. Economist Robert Gordon believes there is good reason to be sceptical, pointing out that US productivity growth has slowed sharply in the past 50 years, compared to the rate of growth between 1870 and 1970. Gordon (2016) attributes this slowdown to a lack of technological advancement, with no disruptive innovation coming close to the transformations brought by commercial electricity, the internal combustion engine, refrigeration and the telephone.

We've gone some way to explaining why it's important to better understand management theories and where they came from. But, those theories already get extensive coverage in management textbooks. So why do we need this book to look again at them?

The questionable representation of management theories in textbooks

There's a game you might have played called 'telephone'. Players form a line and the first person whispers a message in the ear of the second person, who repeats the message to the next person, and so on. The final person announces the message to the group and this is compared with the original message. Typically, the message at the end is different from that at the beginning, often amusingly so. Sometimes players make errors in the retelling and unintentionally pass on a different message. And sometimes they deliberately change the message.

There's a similar dynamic at play regarding how theories are represented in management textbooks. The ideas the theorists originally developed and wrote about are often quite different from what students are presented with. How does this happen? We believe the management misrepresentation game works much like 'telephone', with the message being distorted by both unintentional and intentional actions.

We don't want to be overly critical of textbook authors. Writing textbooks requires enormous effort because authors need to provide a broad overview of the field. Hundreds or even thousands of studies need to be included. Space considerations and the need to present these theories in a way that students can understand means that complex ideas are condensed and simplified. This inevitably means the nuances and caveats presented in the original get lost in the process of translation.

In addition, given the breadth of textbook coverage, it is probably unrealistic to expect textbook authors to have read all the original sources. They might have borrowed and adapted representations of these foundational ideas from other textbooks or from histories of the field written by others. Just like in the 'telephone' game, errors are perpetuated in the retelling and the repeated message becomes increasingly distant from the original.

It's unsurprising, then, that misrepresentations flourish. A good illustration of this is research on emotions. Lisa Feldman Barrett (2017) is a leading neuroscientist who has put forward a theory of how emotions are made in the brain that challenges the commonly-held theory that emotions are like inner beasts that need to be controlled by rational thought. The 'inner beast' theory is based on Charles Darwin's ideas on natural selection and says that emotions are inherited through natural selection and are located in particular parts of the brain that trigger reactions in your body. So, if you see something scary, a 'fear circuit' in your brain will cause your heart rate to increase. This theory interprets our behaviour as a battle taking place in our brains between parts that control emotion and others that control our cognition. It's the theory embedded in the children's movie *Inside Out*, where Joy, Sadness, Fear, Disgust and Anger are individual characters competing to influence the actions of Riley. It's also reflected in legal systems which hold that in crimes of passion, where people are taken over by emotion, they are partly absolved of responsibility.

Barrett has developed an alternative explanation based on her laboratory studies. She argues that we cannot be at the mercy of animalistic emotions that battle against our rational thoughts because the brain does not have separate systems for emotion and cognition. Rather, emotions are constructed by brain-wide networks working together. Barrett believed her theory was novel until she stumbled across some academic papers from the 1930s, 1940s and 1950s, which made the same argument. While those researchers did not have access to her sophisticated neuro-technology, they concluded there was insufficient evidence to support the classical 'inner beast' theory. Mysteriously, this research never made its way into psychology textbooks.

As part of her detective work, Barrett read the original works of Darwin and of William James, the so-called founders of the classical approach. What she found shocked her. Darwin says virtually nothing about natural selection and James was actually arguing *against* the idea that is conventionally attributed to him. Barrett concludes that these misrepresentations of Darwin and James have endured for a century. This matters because companies like Facebook, Google, Apple and Microsoft have spent billions developing software to read the signs of people's emotion, based on the classical view. It also matters because generations of students have been taught a fallacy.

We had a similar experience some years ago when we set out to find what Kurt Lewin wrote about the unfreeze–change–refreeze model of organizational change, probably the most popular theory in change management today. We've taught the model for years but had never been able to find Lewin's original writing on the theory. After an exhaustive search, we discovered he wrote very little about it and presented it differently to what textbooks attribute to him. As we explain in Chapter 5, the three-step organizational change model that we associate with Lewin was developed by others after his death and has been used to promote a top-down, leader-knows-best approach to changing organizations that has little resemblance to Lewin's idea.

Another set of misrepresentations that we have uncovered concerns Maslow's hierarchy of needs pyramid, likely the most famous symbol in management studies. As we discuss in Chapter 3, Maslow did not create the pyramid, and the criticisms textbooks routinely make of his theory were anticipated and accounted for in the 1943 article where he developed his hierarchy of needs. What started as a quite complex theory of human motivation has become a simplistic model that looks great in PowerPoint and is easy for students to remember. But it is not what Maslow created.

We don't expect many students to have read Maslow's 1943 article. The reality is that for most students of management (and we suspect many lecturers), their access to the field's foundational theories is via secondary sources and textbooks. That makes textbooks really important artefacts (Carroll et al., 2018). As we have discussed, we think much of the misrepresentation is unintentional. Textbook authors are required to condense and simplify theories for students, and just like in any reduction, elements of the original are inevitably lost. But just like in the game of 'telephone', there also seems to have been purposeful efforts to distort the original message in ways their creators would not have foreseen and been happy with.

The politics of knowledge about management

To explain this, we need to understand a little about how management as a field of study has developed. Management courses are now often the largest classes at university, but this was not always the case. Compared with long-established disciplines like psychology, sociology, anthropology and political studies, which have existed in various forms for centuries, management studies is young. Its birth is often traced (mistakenly, as we shall argue in Chapter 2) to Frederick Winslow Taylor's book *The Principles of Scientific Management* published in 1911.

Management schools have fought hard (and successfully) to establish themselves in universities and to be considered serious academic subjects with their own body of knowledge that can be taught to students. Like any credible academic subject, management needed a history. The first management histories that attempted to capture the whole field were written in the middle of the twentieth century, as the field itself became more structured and professionalized. There weren't many 'management theorists' at the time, so to build these foundations these writers adapted theories from other disciplines, such as social psychology, like in the case of Maslow's hierarchy of needs. That is important to keep in mind, because it meant these theorists and their ideas needed to be translated for an audience of management students. Maslow was not writing about management, yet his theory is now regarded as a management theory. Just like in the game of telephone, there's a risk of the message being distorted when it is passed from one person to another (or in this case, from one academic field to another). Incorporating already well-known theorists from other disciplines into the management canon lent academic credibility to the fledgling field. However, it has resulted in some misrepresentation of the original theories.

As the numbers of students enrolling in management schools grew, so did the demand for textbooks. Most of the best-selling management textbooks of today were first published in the late 1970s and early 1980s. The few textbooks that preceded them (such as Koontz and O'Donnell, 1955; McFarland, 1958; Terry, 1956) looked nothing like what we associate with textbooks today. Their pages were filled with text, with few if any diagrams, photographs, cases, glossaries or sample questions. In short, they were not 'student-friendly'. However, advances in publishing technology enabled a new kind of textbook that occupied a middle ground between being easy for students to read and maintaining academic credibility. In these new textbooks, the subject of management was divided into discrete chapters, such as motivation, organizational design and managing change. In each sub-field different theories and ideas would be presented, generally chronologically, to show there had been progress. Each chapter would also include exercises or cases studies where students could test their knowledge by applying the theories. Diagrams, particularly ones divided into steps like Maslow's pyramid, made the subject look practically applicable and the knowledge easily testable.

We've talked a bit about how today's best-selling management textbooks came about. Now let's turn our attention to what the purpose of a management textbook is. Most people who read them are taking courses as part of a qualification – so the textbook has an important role in providing students with knowledge of management. Students can then be assessed on that knowledge and, hopefully, they demonstrate that sufficiently to gain the qualification.

But writers of textbooks generally have a purpose beyond that, which you'll often get an insight into if you read the preface at the front of the book. Stoner (1982), author of the world's best-selling textbook at the start of the 1980s, when most of today's best-sellers produced their early editions, articulates this well. Stoner wanted not just to write a book *about* management, but to write a book *for* management.

> I have attempted in this book to convey the very positive view I have of the manager's job...
>
> I have chosen to address the reader as a potential manager. At times, in fact, I even adopt a tone that suggests the reader already is a manager. This is done intentionally: I want to encourage the reader to start thinking like a manager as soon as possible. (Stoner, 1982: xv)

Most management textbooks share Stoner's view that students study management to prepare them for a future role as a manager. That explains why most management textbooks are written from the perspective of the manager, presenting knowledge as something to be applied by managers to improve the productivity of employees and the profitability of organizations. To return to our example of Maslow, from this perspective learning about the hierarchy of needs is valuable because we can use it to better manage staff motivation.

While there is nothing wrong with a managerialist perspective *per se*, it is worth understanding how this perspective influences what theories are included in management textbooks and how they are presented. We've touched on the examples of Maslow and Lewin already, and we explore these and other theories throughout this book. But the managerialist perspective also influences what theories are *excluded* from textbooks, and we will explore examples of this also.

These decisions about inclusion and exclusion, as well as decisions about how to present the original work of theorists in simplified form for students, are influenced by value judgements. These value judgements are subjective (there is no right or wrong approach) and they are, in part, political judgements. This point is made by a number of well-established textbook authors in a 2003 article 'Management textbooks as propaganda', published in *Journal of Management Education*. They were asked: 'Do you see your textbooks as propaganda or ideology?' Propaganda was defined as 'material disseminated to convert from one belief, doctrine, or faith to another'; ideology as 'the body of ideas reflecting the social needs and aspirations of a particular individual, group, class, or culture' (Cameron et al., 2003: 713). Probably the best-selling and most influential management textbook author, Stephen Robbins, responded:

> I see my books as supporting an ideology. But, of course, all text-books sell an ideology. [Organizational Behaviour] books ... for the most part, support a managerial perspective. This reflects the market – business schools. We need to genuflect to the Gods of productivity, efficiency, goals, etc. This strongly influences the dependent variables researchers choose and the ones that text-book authors use. So we reflect business school values. (Robbins, in Cameron et al., 2003: 714)

The managerial perspective/ideology articulated above emphasizes hierarchical power relations, privileges the role of managers and sees efficiency, performance and profitability as the ends to which organizational activity should be directed. Robbins argues that supporting this ideology is appropriate as the purpose of management education is to train future managers. Textbooks, therefore, are not just tools that assist universities in granting qualifications in management; they also play an influential role in socializing students into a managerial worldview.

So what's the problem? Being trained to think like and act like a manager may well have been the reason you enrolled in a management course. But it is the dominance of this singular perspective that we take issue with in this book. Aside from the dubious assertion that students can be trained in a practical activity (managing) by reading textbooks and sitting in large lecture theatres (as opposed to learning 'on the job'), looking from the perspective of the manager is just *one* way of understanding behaviour in organizations.

Another way is to look from the perspective of those who are managed, which we could call the 'employee perspective'. Relatively few students, especially at undergraduate level, will have been managers, but many have been employees, and studying the subject from that perspective can provide different, valuable insights. Whereas the 'managerial perspective' may value efficiency, productivity and profit, the 'employee perspective' might value justice, fairness, autonomy and equality. That's not to say the managerial perspective isn't interested in these, but it's probably only interested when the pursuit of them is consistent with its objectives of performance and profitability.

You might have come across the term 'business case' in discussions of topics like diversity. This is the idea that having more diverse organizations, across dimensions such as gender, ethnicity, age, etc. makes sense from a business perspective (which generally means it is a profit-maximizing strategy) because diverse people bring different ideas, perspectives and experiences that benefit the business. Because the business case of diversity has been proven, diversity has now become accepted into the managerialist perspective of management. But shouldn't having diverse organizations where people are given equal opportunities to succeed be seen as a desirable end in itself? That is important from a perspective that values equality and fairness above profit. Both are useful perspectives to consider.

As we will see later in the book, some ideas from the employee perspective, such as giving employees more voice in major issues affecting the business, are yet to have reached the status of a proven business case. Therefore, they tend to be excluded from textbooks. So, if textbooks present the managerialist view as the only view, students are only getting one side of the story.

There's another problem with the way most management textbooks present the field's foundational theories. Kim Cameron, a best-selling textbook author in leadership, was asked the same question as Robbins: 'Do you see your textbooks as propaganda or ideology?' Cameron agreed that management textbooks were propaganda publications (in terms of privileging the managerial worldview), but he saw that as legitimate provided textbooks included only research that met the highest scientific standards, 'Persuading students to believe in the truth – no matter how propaganda-like – is still a virtue' (Cameron et al., 2003: 720).

Management textbooks like to highlight their scientific credentials. For example, Nelson and Quick's *Organizational Behavior* textbook is subtitled *Science, the Real World, and You*. In the preface, the authors note:

Science refers to the broad and deep research roots of our discipline. Our book is anchored in research tradition and contains classic research and leading-edge scholarship in the field. (Nelson and Quick, 2013: xxiii)

We are sceptical about this for two reasons. First, many of the theories that appear in best-selling textbooks, such as Maslow's hierarchy of needs, have produced disappointing results in scientific studies, as we detail in Chapter 4. Second, we've noticed that not all 'classic research' gets included in textbooks. In Chapter 6 we discuss Stanley Milgram's famous obedience experiments. Milgram, a social psychologist, ran a series of experiments in the 1960s that highlighted the dangers of following orders given by people in authority. These receive extensive coverage in social psychology textbooks but are often absent from organizational behaviour textbooks, including Nelson and Quick (2013).

We think that's got something to do with Milgram's findings not being consistent with the managerial perspective. Most management textbooks encourage students to obey their bosses, not disobey them, so it's no surprise that Milgram's experiments are often excluded. That is a great pity, given the potential for a university education to help students develop their critical thinking skills and intellectual independence.

The aims of this book

We haven't painted a very flattering picture of conventional management textbooks. But, as we said earlier, we don't want to be overly critical of authors, because textbooks take an enormous amount of effort to write. For the past decade we've been publishing research (listed in the Appendix) that explores the origins of well-known theories of management and how these might be better presented to students. Some textbook authors have reached out and encouraged us to work with them to develop alternative presentations. This suggests that there is a growing appetite and a demand for a new approach, such as the one we promote in this book.

While we have written this book for use on university courses, it is not a conventional textbook. Chris Grey (2005), who inspired this book series, saw a need for books that were written for students, but which did not reproduce the standard textbook format – books that were very short (rather than long), reasonably cheap (unlike most textbooks) and fairly interesting. By design and in keeping with the intent of this series, this book is not comprehensive. We discuss many of management's most well-known theorists, but there are many that we do not include. This is partly because this is a 'very short' series, but also because we feel it is better to focus on a smaller number of theories in depth. Having talked to numerous employers, we know they don't expect graduates with management qualifications to have memorized 10 theories of motivation, for example. They hope they might have a basic understanding of how thinking about motivation has developed over time, but what they value is generic graduate skills that are needed in most jobs – communication skills, analytical skills, an ability to look at old problems in new ways, and the ability to think critically.

A critical orientation is a distinctive feature of the 'very short, fairly interesting' book series. It is reflected in the approach we take to exploring management's foundational theories, where we challenge the way these theories are conventionally represented in best-selling management textbooks. This approach is informed by an important distinction – between 'the past' and 'history', which we want to take some time now to explain.

The conventional view of 'history' is to see it as a factual, objective account of what happened in the past, why it happened and who was important in making it happen. This view suggests that while we can (and should) learn from history to avoid repeating the mistakes of the past, we should not change or 're-write' history. We challenge this view by distinguishing between 'the past' and 'history' (Jenkins, 2003). We see the 'past' as events that have occurred already, with 'history' being a narrative of those past events – the connection we have to the past which we can draw on to make sense of both the present and the future. If you accept this distinction, you must also accept that history is a subjective account of the past. As we have discussed already with regard to textbooks, those who produce history make decisions about which events from the past to highlight and therefore which to relegate to a minor mention or omit altogether. They make decisions about which people (or characters in the narrative) to give prominence to, and which to assign a minor role or exclude. While we acknowledge the producer of the history has a responsibility to weigh up the evidence in making these judgements, in the end they are subjective, rather than objective judgements. The past cannot speak for itself.

One way of describing the aim of this book then is to see it as an alternative history of management theory. Our approach has been informed by the work of Michel Foucault, a French intellectual who is often described as a postmodernist, or poststructuralist, but whom we regard as a critical historian. Foucault wrote histories that challenged conventional historical accounts. These conventional histories aimed to provide the truth about 'what really happened', but also presented a narrative of progress towards the superior knowledge of today. Foucault saw conventional histories as providing legitimacy for those in power, which had the effect of shutting down alternative ways of understanding the past. He was especially interested in understanding how relations of power constructed and supported fields of knowledge and how this affected what happened in the present.

Foucault didn't set out to uncover the 'real truth', but to examine how this truth and the assumptions related to it came to be taken for granted, and, through this, to raise doubts about what is promoted as the truth. Foucault developed an approach called 'genealogy', which focused on how webs of connection and power constructed and supported the formation of truths. He also saw that what was promoted as 'the truth' had particular effects – some people and groups gained, while others lost out. Typically, it was those in powerful positions who gained, and those less powerful that suffered. Some examples of this from his most famous works include:

- Foucault's studies of psychology and psychiatry's status as sciences and their promotion of the modern view that sanity, or what is normal, is an objective, pre-existing condition and that we can therefore classify some people as normal and others as not (Foucault, 1985); and
- His genealogy of punishment, which critiqued the assumption that prisons are the most humane way of punishing criminals. Foucault countered that prisons were part of a complex system by which modern societies 'disciplined' citizens and workers in ways that made them more docile and compliant – all of which maximized their productivity (Foucault, 1979). We say more about this in Chapter 3.

We have followed a similar process in exploring the presentation of management theories in textbooks. We began with the question 'why do management textbooks represent theories as they do?' and question the normal responses 'because it's a good representation of what those theorists actually wrote' or 'because it is the best way of educating our students'.

It is important to note that authors are not the only ones who shape the content of textbooks. Also influential were those who wrote the first histories of management, such as George (1968) and Wren (1972) that textbooks authors drew from. Textbook publishers are also influential. We've been told by a leading textbook author that it is common for publishers to employ content developers who decide what should be included (and therefore excluded) from textbooks. We explore through a series of examples how the network of theorists, historians, textbook authors, publishers and others have produced what we conventionally assume to be the body of management theory. We examine who gains by these theories being understood in the way they are and who loses.

This process of questioning the way management theories are typically presented in textbooks is a creative activity. If we accept the distinction between the past and history, then we are freer to create new histories of the past that shine a light on people, places and ideas that have been ignored or forgotten by history. For example, we can see Maslow not as the architect of a flawed pyramid, but as someone who saw freedom of expression as a precondition for the satisfaction of human needs at work. And if we better understand what Lewin actually wrote about change in organizations (e.g., that the approach to change that met with most success involved all stakeholders working collaboratively and agreeing on the way forward), we can create different foundation stones for managing change than the simplistic unfreeze–change–refreeze theory uncritically attributed to him.

By looking differently at the past, we can be creative in opening new ways of thinking about management and managing, in response to the challenges we face today and into the future.

How the book is organized

We hope this book will be used to teach management and so have structured it much like a regular management textbook, with chapters focusing on major topics. At the end of each chapter we identify 'critical insights'. These summarize what can be learnt by thinking critically about theories that are typically included in best-selling textbooks, as well as from theories that are often excluded.

In Chapter 2 we focus on theorists that are introduced early on in management textbooks, including Adam Smith, Max Weber, Frederick Taylor and Mary Parker Follett. We discuss the typical textbook coverage of these theories and why we might want to question those assumed foundations.

The conventional account of management's evolution tells the story of a shift away from the dark days of scientific management to an enlightened period of 'human relations', which places employees' social needs at the forefront of managers' thinking. In Chapter 3 we discuss influential theories of motivation. We also argue that the conventional historical account obscures a dark side, where employees are motivated as much by fear and constant surveillance as opportunities to fulfil social needs.

Chapter 4 introduces theories of personality, group dynamics and culture, and analyses how they are generally described by management textbooks. We introduce alternative theories which suggest that matching personalities to jobs and creating cohesive group and organizational cultures can stifle independent thought, innovation and creativity.

Chapter 5 explores theories of leadership and change, which are inextricably linked. We show how today's popular personality-based leadership theories are largely a repackaging of discredited ideas from the past. There were good reasons why these approaches fell out of favour – those who possessed the desired personality characteristics were sometimes narcissists with disturbing visions. Personality-based leadership is at the heart of well-known theories of change and is contributing, we argue, to increasing change fatigue and cynicism.

In Chapter 6 we focus on ethics and corporate social responsibility (CSR). We argue that while ethical theories promote an ideal of the ethical manager, they ignore important aspects of ethics, such as the role of government. We also challenge the conventional textbook portrayal of ethics and CSR as being new topics, showing debates about the morality of business executives and the responsibilities of business to be much older. Analyzing this past provides insight into how we might address current challenges.

Finally, in our concluding chapter, we reflect on the value of questioning the representation of theories in management textbooks. We outline our hope that textbooks might change for the better while acknowledging that change will not be easy. We also draw together the 20 critical insights developed in the book into one summary table on pages 123–4, to make it easier for you to revise the contents.

Ultimately, we hope that our stories of management theory's past will inspire innovation. We hope they encourage you to think anew about what management is and how it can be practised differently (and better) in the future. We concur with a statement often attributed to Lewin, but most likely never actually said by him: 'There is nothing so practical as a good theory.'

2

The Classical School: Looking Again at the Foundations of Management Theory

This is Chapter 2, which is significant because in almost every management textbook, Chapter 2 is where management's foundational theories are explained. There is a reinforcing pattern to the arrangement. Chapter 1 is where 'management' is defined. Chapter 2 shows how that particular view emerged over time. Then, the subsequent chapters outline how progress from this point of origin has been made in the various traditional sub-fields of management, such as motivation, group dynamics and leadership. The final chapters are on what are regarded as new or contemporary topics like ethics, sustainability and innovation – topics that we assume our forebears did not consider.

The problem is, as with most attempts to package up a history into a tidy narrative that confirms a particular view of the present, that while we live life in all its complexity forwards, we understand it backwards. To paraphrase Danish philosopher Soren Kierkegaard, we make sense of the past in hindsight, looking for and subsequently finding simplistic linear causes and effects.

As we noted in Chapter 1, the first histories of management were written in the middle of the twentieth century and the way they were written reflected the view of what management was perceived to be at that time. Management was about achieving greater efficiency, the desired outputs were assumed to be financial, and the organizations where managers worked were drawn as triangle-shaped hierarchies. Those first histories looked back to see where the present had come from. And it was those histories that provided the material from which textbook writers in the 1970s and 1980s built their Chapter 2s. The most popular of those textbooks continue to this day (often in their 18th, 19th or even 20th editions), and because their history chapters have hardly changed, those views of what management is fundamentally about remain largely unchallenged too.

In this chapter, we look again and with a different lens at the early (or classical) theories of management: Frederick Taylor and scientific management; Adam Smith, who is seen to have laid the groundwork for free market capitalism, the industrial revolution and scientific management's focus on efficiency; Max Weber and his supposed advocacy of the bureaucratic organizational form; and Mary Parker Follett, who is later inserted into the very male history of management as its 'mother' or 'prophet'. We focus on these theories with a broader view, to show that they can be interpreted in ways that can help us think differently and innovatively about the management challenges we face now, rather than limit us by reinforcing old stereotypes about how much smarter *we* are now and how much simpler *they* were back then.

Frederick Winslow Taylor and Scientific Management

The date that many prescribe as the starting point of management is 1911. This is because: 'That's the year Frederick W. Taylor's *Principles of Scientific Management* was published. His ground-breaking book described a theory of scientific management' (Robbins et al., 2016: 27).

Taylor (1856–1915) was born into a wealthy Philadelphia family. Rather than follow his father into the legal profession, he ended up in the steel industry. He began as an apprentice and then worked as a labourer and machinist, first at Midvale Steel Works and then at Bethlehem Steel. Taylor believed that employers and employees shared a common goal of creating successful businesses. However, he felt that both sides were stuck in an adversarial mindset which resulted in huge inefficiency. Employers tried to drive down wages where they could, believing that this would increase profits, while workers only produced about one third of what they were capable of producing. This was partly due to laziness (what Taylor called 'natural soldiering') but partly due to workers deliberately restricting output in order not to do themselves or their workmates out of a job (what he called 'systematic soldiering'). Many workers were paid a fixed amount per day, which meant they received the same amount regardless of their level of output. Those who were on 'piece work' had seen that if they increased their output, then management would often reduce the payment per piece. Taylor believed that a third cause of low productivity was poor work methods. Knowledge about how tasks should be carried out had been passed down by workers through the generations and these methods were inefficient – they did not maximize the potential of the person or the machinery they were using.

The 'maximum prosperity' that Taylor sought could only be achieved by a radical redesign of the way work was done to maximize the output of both the workers and machines. His new approach (1911: 36–7) consisted of four management principles:

'First. Develop a science for each element of a man's work [to determine the one best way. This] replaces the old rule-of-thumb method.' [Ostensibly, 'science' means here develop a time and motion study to determine the most efficient division of labour and work processes for doing the work.]

'Second. Scientifically select and then train, teach, and develop the workman, whereas in the past he chose his own work and trained himself as best he could.'

'Third. Heartily cooperate with the men so as to insure all of the work being done [is] in accordance with the principles of the science which has been developed.'

'Fourth. There is an almost equal division of the work and the responsibility between the management and the workmen. The management take over all work for which they are better fitted than the workmen' [which means that managers do all the planning, directing and controlling of the work and the workers do the work].

Taylor illustrated the potential of his principles by conducting an experiment at Bethlehem Steel with a Dutch worker he called Schmidt. Schmidt was a pig-iron handler – his job consisted of picking up a 'pig' of iron (a measure that weighed 92 pounds or 41 kilograms), walking up a plank and dropping it into a railroad car. Taylor observed that Schmidt and his co-workers were loading about 12.5 ton per day. Taylor believed that if he scientifically re-designed the work to maximize the efficiency of the task and if he paid Schmidt more, he could generate a significant increase in output. Taylor selected Schmidt for his study for his strength and fitness (he would run to work in the morning and run home in the evening), and because he needed extra money for a house he was building. Curiously, it also seems Schmidt was an attractive choice for Taylor because he was 'mentally sluggish' (Taylor, 1911: 46) and would focus on the money and not on how hard he was going to have to work. Under scientific management, managers did the 'thinking' and 'workers' did the 'doing'. Taylor preferred workers who didn't think too much.

Taylor offered Schmidt $1.85 per day (much more than his current rate of $1.15) and told Schmidt he must do exactly what his manager instructs him.

When he tells you to pick up a pig and walk, you pick it up and you walk, and when he tells you to sit down and rest, you sit down. You do that right straight through the day. And what's more, no back talk. (1911: 46)

Schmidt agreed. The next day he loaded 47.5 tons and, according to Taylor, he maintained that level of production for the next three years. Taylor's experiment had demonstrated the huge potential of scientific management to increase efficiency and productivity.

Scientific Management revolutionizes the automobile industry

At the turn of the twentieth century, the workers who produced engines belonged to craft unions. They had control over the way the work was done and the speed at which it was done. Car manufacturers took pride in how their skilled craftsmen worked slowly and carefully to construct vehicles with their hands. The process took weeks and the workers took pride in what they had created, even though the labour-intensive process meant that those who built the cars could rarely afford to buy them. This changed when Henry Ford developed his Model T. To make the cars affordable for the masses, Ford needed to produce them more efficiently and he was interested in the buzz surrounding scientific management.

In keeping with Taylor's principles, Ford reorganized car production into simple, repetitive steps, which meant there was no longer a need for skilled craftsmen. Workers could be easily trained to do any job, with tasks like making a wheel, previously done by one person, broken down into 100 stages, done by different men using different machines. Each car was built from the ground up on stationary wooden stands. Ford then had an even better idea – instead of moving workers around the car, why not keep the workers in one place and move the car past them. It was the birth of the moving assembly line.

The efficiency gains were enormous, but the nature of the work had been transformed. Work that was highly skilled became low skilled. Workers went from being in control of the speed they worked at to being dictated by the speed of the production line, which was controlled by management. The Model T was hugely profitable for Ford, so to win over the workers to his new production methods, he offered to double wages to $5 a day. He was overrun with eager applicants but the enthusiasm was short-lived. The mood is captured by Charlie Chaplin in his 1936 film *Modern Times*, which opens with his Little Tramp character working on a factory production line. As workers pour into the steel factory at the start of the day, the manager (seated at his desk and engrossed in a jigsaw puzzle) pauses to issue an order that the production line be sped up. Charlie, who has the monotonous task of tightening nuts as they whizz past him on the line, has a miserable existence, constantly berated by the foreman standing over him.

If you have studied an introduction to management course, the story we have told of Taylor and Schmidt may well be familiar to you – it is part of management studies' folklore. You might also be familiar with the story of Henry Ford's application of scientific management, nicely told in the PBS documentary *On the Line* (1924). Scientific management, the story goes, became popular because business owners, like Henry Ford, wanted greater efficiency.

What has largely been forgotten, however, is that scientific management might never have gained popularity had it not been for conservationists – people who were concerned with reducing the wasteful use of non-renewable resources, or what we might today call 'sustainability'. Understanding this forgotten past can get us thinking about a different legacy for scientific management, as we explore in the next section.

A new history of Scientific Management

In a best-selling book called *This Changes Everything: Capitalism versus the Climate* (2017), activist Naomi Klein argued that our current age faces a never-before-seen collision between forces for capitalism and ecological concerns. While we concur with Klein that this clash is real, the idea that we have never encountered it before, and, relatedly, that today's focus on sustainability and the environmental impacts of management are things that only our modern age has been mindful enough to see, is not so real. In fact, this clash is a key foundation that led to the formation of management studies. What Klein's unknowingly false assertion illustrates is that we don't have a particularly accurate or broad view of management's past, and that if we did, we might have more ideas at our disposal that we could deploy to confront today's challenges, because they have been confronted by some very intelligent people before.

Management textbooks focus on Taylor when they cover scientific management because it is assumed that he developed and popularized it. But, in fact, it became popular because of a particular problem: how to control the development of big business running amok in the United States. Theodore Roosevelt became President in 1901 at a pivotal moment: a transition from the Gilded Age to the Progressive Era. His progressive agenda put him on a collision course with the 'heroes' of the Gilded Age's rapid industrial expansion, such as Andrew Carnegie and J.P. Morgan. By the end of 1906, influential business interests in the West of the US and conservatives in the East were organizing against Roosevelt's attempts to curb the industrial growth that, in their minds, was a key part of the 'American Dream'.

Roosevelt needed to convince the public that government should rein in the free market capitalism that was destroying the natural environment and tearing at the country's social fabric. One of his advisors, Gifford Pinchot, who had responsibility for the forestry sector, suggested to Roosevelt that he focus on what he called 'conservation' – the active management of scarce resources for future generations. While the seed of the conservation movement may have been planted as a particular project relating to forests, Roosevelt succeeded in popularizing conservation as the biggest issue of the time.

Once Roosevelt's term as President ended in 1909, his conservation agenda became vulnerable, but it was kept in the news by a Progressive lawyer from Boston named Louis D. Brandeis. While his moniker 'the people's lawyer' related to his being *for* the interests of ordinary people *against* the special interests of big business, it also reflected Brandeis' ability to skilfully market the causes he was representing through the media to get public opinion onside.

In 1910, Brandeis worked on the case that led to the development of management as an important field of study: the Eastern Rate Case (ERC). The Eastern Railroad Company wanted to put their prices up. Brandeis, representing the company's corporate customers, argued that this rate hike was unfair and would put them out of business. Brandeis argued that if the railroads reduced waste through new production practices, then the rates could stay as they were and the railroads' bottom-line could even grow. To make this case, he assembled a group of industrial experts. This group included Henry Gantt (inventor of the Gantt chart) and Frank Gilbreth, who with wife Lillian raised twelve children using scientific management principles. Their son Frank Gilbreth Jnr and daughter Ernestine Carey wrote about their childhood in *Cheaper by the Dozen* (1948), which was subsequently made into multiple Hollywood movies. Gantt and Gilbreth had read Taylor's 1903 book *Shop Management* and were keen to get him involved. Brandeis liked Taylor's ideas too but not the names Taylor had given them: the Taylor System, Shop Management, Functional Management. So, Brandeis created a new one designed to win over the public and win the case – Scientific Management.

Initially, Taylor wasn't keen to be involved. He did not like the term scientific management and was feeling frustrated that his efficiency system had not been as popular as he had hoped. But his mood changed when he saw the publicity Brandeis generated. The headline of the

New York Times on November 21, 1910 read: 'RAILROADS COULD SAVE $1,000,000 A DAY: Brandeis says Scientific Management Would Do It' (Copley, 1923). Brandeis, with the eventual help of Taylor, ended up winning the case and the following year wrote up his ideas in the first book published on scientific management, *Scientific Management and Railroads* (Brandeis, 1911). The book's first line reads 'The efficiency movement, of which scientific management is an important factor, expresses a new philosophy that conceives of conservation as the central motive in the conduct of industry' (1911: 4).

While it may seem far-fetched today to believe that conservation gave management studies wings, further evidence for this appears in the first line of Taylor's book, published later that year: 'President Roosevelt, in his address to the Governors at the White House, prophetically remarked that "The conservation of our national resources is only preliminary to the larger question of national efficiency", (Taylor, 1911: 1). The growth of the conservation movement inspired Taylor and gave him new purpose. It was not only natural resources such as forests, coal and iron that was going to waste, but, Taylor realized, 'our larger wastes of human effort' (1911: 1).

Why conventional management history overlooks the conservation movement

If the link between conservation and scientific management was once clearly understood, why do we not see it now? And why do we regard Taylor as a 'founding father' of management and not Brandeis? Brandeis went on to great things (he became a Justice of the Supreme Court in 1916), but his crowning achievements were in the field of law and he had little interest in becoming a leader in the field of management. Also, Taylor, before he died in 1915, had attracted a group of followers who worked as consultants implementing his principles. These consultants had an interest in seeing Taylor's reputation enhanced.

So, when the first histories of management were written by George, Chandler and Wren in the middle of the twentieth century, Taylor was a more attractive choice of founder than Brandeis. It made sense to have an engineering consultant as the central figure in the narrative rather than a lawyer. These histories focused on the *what* of Taylor's efficiency idea and not on the *how* and *why* it came to be. They informed the management textbook industry in the 1970s and 1980s, when the first editions of many of today's popular textbooks were drafted. The conservation movement that had burned so brightly under Roosevelt was forgotten.

Why does this matter? The idea that management studies originated from a concern about the rampant development of big business and that conservation was the solution, seems far-fetched now. But by understanding this alternative origin story, we may be encouraged to see management differently. What if Roosevelt and Brandeis were taught as management pioneers? What if the aim of management today was as it was defined 100 years ago – the greatest good for the greatest number for the longest time? We might avoid claims like that made by Naomi Klein that we are seeing for the first time the clash between capitalism and the environment. We would understand that a concern with sustainability, which many assume to be a recent development, was where management studies began.

As we will explore in the following chapter, scientific management has developed a bad reputation in management textbooks, for creating dull jobs that crushes the human spirit. These criticisms are justified, but we should remember that there is more to scientific management than that and there are aspects that can help us face today's challenges. For instance, we might apply scientific management to improve food harvesting techniques, as well as the storing, transporting, packaging and selling of food. The theory might help us address the problem of up to 30 per cent of the food we produce being wasted. This accounts for up to 10 per cent of global greenhouse gas emissions, according to the Intergovernmental Panel on Climate Change (Irfan, 2019). Zero waste is not a new idea. It was a founding theory that has been forgotten by management's history.

Adam Smith: ethics before economics

We talked in the introductory chapter about how management studies fought to be taken seriously in universities among more established fields, such as psychology and economics. It was important to have a history of the field that connected to great thinkers from the past. One figure called upon to make the history of management grander is the famous economist Adam Smith (1723–1790).

Smith isn't just important for the history of management. His 1776 book, *The Wealth of Nations*, is widely regarded as the foundation stone of economics. Even if you haven't studied economics or management, you might have heard about Smith, because his name is regularly invoked to justify a free-market or laissez-faire version of capitalism that opposes government intervention in business affairs. In *The Wealth of Nations*, Smith stated that:

> It is not from the benevolence of the butcher, the brewer, or the baker, that we expect our dinner, but from their regard to their own interest. We address ourselves, not to their humanity but to their self-love, and never talk to them of our own necessities but of their advantages. (*The Wealth of Nations*, 1776/2012: I.ii.2)

The lesson generally derived from this passage is that if business people pursue their self-interest in business – if they seek to maximize their profits – then collectively, we will all be better off. Smith talked of society being 'led by an invisible hand' that guides the free market to produce outcomes that benefit everyone (*The Wealth of Nations*, 1776/2012: IV.ii.9).

These ideas have implications for the role of government in a capitalist system. If the 'invisible hand' of the market benefits everyone, then government should not seek to restrict these market forces, however well-intentioned it might be in wanting to alleviate inequality or other social issues. In the opening chapter, we discussed how conventional management textbooks promote managerial values – productivity and efficiency, but also, we suggest, profit-maximization and free-market capitalism. It is easy to see why having a stamp of approval from a major historical figure like Smith would be attractive to economics and management studies.

In management textbooks, Smith is also credited for being the first to develop the concept of the division of labour, or what we might call job specialization. This idea of breaking jobs into narrow, repetitive tasks was picked up by Frederick Taylor for his theory of scientific management. In *The Wealth of Nations*, Smith draws on the example of a pin factory to show that workers performing all the operations to produce a pin by themselves could produce a tiny fraction of the pins that they could if each specialized in only one or two of the tasks. This was because specialized workers get skilled at their narrow tasks and can perform them quickly. Also, they do not waste time transitioning from one task to another and are more likely to discover more efficient methods.

Smith is an important historical figure for business schools, especially in management studies and economics. However, this Smith is a very simplified cartoon version of the reality. Historical accounts focus narrowly on some of his ideas to the exclusion of others and provide little insight into *how* Smith came to these ideas and why. Influential mid-twentieth-century management historians argued that Smith 'advocated laissez-faire capitalism' (Wren, 1972: 23; see also George, 1972). But Smith never used this term in his own writing and opposed these ideas, which were being advocated by the French writers he critiqued. Smith only mentioned the 'invisible hand' metaphor once in *The Wealth of Nations*. He did not say that self-interest is the one and only principle that matters in human affairs, or even in the economy, and he points out many instances where acting in self-interest can be harmful to society. However, these never seem to get a mention in management and economics textbooks.

Another important point often omitted is that *The Wealth of Nations* wasn't Smith's only book, and probably not what he would have regarded as his most important book. Seventeen years prior, he published *The Theory of Moral Sentiments*, which begins by refuting self-interest, or what his predecessor and mentor, philosopher David Hume, termed the 'selfish hypothesis': 'How selfish soever man may be supposed', Smith writes, 'there are evidently some principles in his nature, which interest him in the fortune of others' (*The Theory of Moral Sentiments*, 1759/2010: I.i.1). Smith states that we sympathize with others by placing ourselves in their shoes. We feel compassion and are naturally compelled to help those we see in difficulty. Others do the same and we achieve mutual enrichment. This theory of moral sentiments was, in Smith's view, how society progresses.

This is a theme Smith develops in *The Wealth of Nations*. Moral sentiment between humans provides the trust necessary for the division of labour to work, because division of labour only works well if we trust others to 'do their bit'. And if they do their bit, we can then trust them to trade, or 'truck and barter' as Smith puts it, fairly. Societies that advance in this way do better than societies that don't.

So, we could say that it is Smith's ethical system of moral sentiments – or mutual sympathy – that is the foundation of management's concept of the division of labour. This would be more in keeping with how Smith is understood by disciplines outside the business school – as a moral philosopher, not as an economist. We should also keep in mind that while Smith is the poster child for free-market capitalism, the whole last book of *The Wealth of Nations* (Book V) is a treatise on how the State should intervene to mitigate the negative effects of an economy where the self-interest of capitalists is given free rein.

Why is the version of Smith that appears in textbooks such a one-sided portrayal of Smith's thinking? A cynical answer is that those who benefitted from an economic system based on self-interest, and those who wanted to build an academic field, picked the bits out of Smith's writing that justified their preferred view and ignored the rest. A more charitable explanation is that when the first histories of management theory were being written in the mid to late twentieth century, writers took their cues from the discipline they looked up to: economics, which, by this point, had already twisted Smith into this simplified version of a nascent neoclassical economics professor.

Max Weber and the shape of an organization

Standing alongside Frederick Taylor and Adam Smith as the most prominent founding fathers of management is German philosopher and sociologist Max Weber (1864–1920). If you read management textbooks, you could be forgiven for thinking Weber was a management theorist, because he is credited with developing bureaucracy theory. This theory of organizing is reflected back to us when we ask students to draw the organization they work for. Most will draw something that looks like the diagram in Figure 2.1, a triangle shape of lines and boxes indicating formal roles and lines of authority – the defining features of the bureaucratic form.

In the 1960s, Alfred Chandler, writing one of the first histories of management, *Strategy and Structure*, drew inspiration from Weber in defining the core features of a business enterprise: 'it contains many distinct operating units and is managed by a hierarchy of salaried executives' (Chandler, 1962: 1, see Figure 2.1). For historians, like Chandler, the brilliant Weber, who had made the investigation of bureaucratic forms such a focus in his work and developed a theory that explained the emergence of the modern corporation, was an obvious foundation stone.

Managements textbooks of the 1970s were also kind to Weber, portraying bureaucracy as a great theory that explained how organizations became more efficient. Then, through the 1980s and 1990s, as the theory fell out of favour, editions of textbooks gradually portray Weber in an increasingly negative light.

Recall the distinction between 'the past' and 'history' that we made in Chapter 1. History is the narrative or story that we construct about the past. It is written in the present and therefore it tends to reflect the concerns of the present. The shifting treatment of Weber by management textbooks is an illustration of this fluidity of history – as attitudes towards bureaucracy changed, so did our understanding of Weber's contribution to management studies.

Today, the textbook portrayal by Schermerhorn et al. (2020) is typical. Weber, we are told, believed that organizations performed below their potential because the people running them had got there because of their family connections or social status, rather than their ability. 'At the heart of Weber's thinking was a specific form of organization he believed could correct the problems just described – bureaucracy' (2020: 41). Weber's 'ideal, intentionally rational and very efficient form of organization' (2020: 41) was founded on the following principles:

- clear division of labour
- clear hierarchy of authority (as illustrated by Figure 2.1)
- formal rules and procedures – decisions are made on the basis of written documents
- impersonality – people are treated according to the rules
- careers based on merit – people are selected and promoted on their ability

Today's textbook narrative is that while Weber sincerely believed bureaucracies would be high-performing organizations, good managers now know they are fundamentally flawed. Bureaucracy is associated with excessive rules or 'red-tape', slowness in adapting to changes in the organization's environment and employee apathy – a poor fit for today's rapidly dynamic (or VUCA) business world, where agility is required (Schermerhorn et al., 2020).

An antidote to bureaucracy is Heckscher's (1994) theory of 'post-bureaucracy'. In Heckscher's 'ideal type', the emphasis on structure is

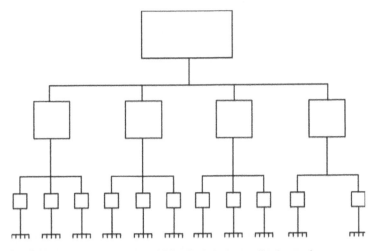

Figure 2.1 A representation of Chandler's bureaucratic shape of an organization

abandoned in favour of relationships, with everyone taking responsibility for organizational performance rather than focusing on their place in the hierarchy. Rules are replaced by dialogue and reaching consensus, tasks are assigned on merit rather than the hierarchy, people are treated as individuals with their particular circumstances considered and the boundaries of the organization are opened.

One manifestation of this theory is in career patterns. Jobs in bureaucracies were considered 'jobs for life', but post-bureaucracies are open to employing outsiders. Advances in technology mean that work need no longer be performed 'on site' or at the office, and it can be done at different times (rather than in the traditional working week of Monday to Friday, 9am to 5pm). And, whereas in bureaucracy structures and rules are considered permanent, in post-bureaucracy there is an expectation of continuous change.

The simplistic narrative of today's best-selling management textbooks is that bureaucracy is bad and post-bureaucracy is good. That Weber was well intentioned, but with the benefit of hindsight we now realize bureaucracies have all these problems he did not foresee.

We don't think that this does justice to Weber's ideas. He was theorizing a shift throughout society in forms of authority, away from traditional authority (we do it this way because that's the way it has always been done) and from charismatic authority (the personal authority of individuals) towards rational-legal authority (that comes from following the rules).

Weber was sure that bureaucratic organization was 'always, from a formal technical point of view, the most rational type', but it exhibited only a 'technical superiority over other forms' (Weber, 1948: 337, 214). He understood why bureaucracy had become popular. At that time, organizations were growing rapidly, which meant they needed to be overseen by professional managers. In addition, Weber believed that bureaucracy suited a culture that was characterized by a 'Protestant Work Ethic' (said to emphasize regular work, discipline, frugality and deferred gratification). However, contrary to what most management textbooks would have us believe, Weber did not see bureaucracy as 'ideal'. He saw its dark side clearly.

Rational calculation [and bureaucratic logic] reduces every worker to a cog in this bureaucratic machine. ... It is horrible to think that the world could one day be filled with nothing but those little cogs, little men clinging to little jobs and striving toward bigger ones – a state of affairs ... playing an ever increasing part in the spirit of our present administrative systems, and especially of its offspring, the students. This passion for bureaucracy is enough to drive one to despair ... the great question is therefore not how we can promote and hasten it, but what can we oppose to this machinery in order to keep a portion of mankind free from [the] supreme mastery of the bureaucratic way of life. (Weber 1909, in Mayer, 1943: 127–8)

Indeed, in the years before today's triangle-shaped organization chart became the norm, other thinkers unencumbered by modern cultural norms saw organization in other ways: as far more individualized, inspirational and organic than what we tend to associate with the industrial era. For example, in 1867, in what was possibly the first modern organization chart, the Erie Railroad Company from New York was depicted as a tree. The board of directors were its roots and its divisions represented as branches extending from the base.

If we were to take Weber seriously as a foundational theorist of management, we should abandon the simplistic narrative that his bureaucracy theory was wrong. We could instead adopt his sociological theory that organizational forms and management approaches are reflective of prevailing beliefs, and if we wish to seek innovations in organization and management we should look to and learn from other cultures. Weber's big management idea was that prominent organizational forms are shaped by culture or the 'spirit of the times'.

Unfortunately, in management writing, the opposite has happened. We have generally tried, with hindsight, to fit other cultures into modern views. So, for example, the structure of Egyptian society will be drawn into layers of a pyramid like an organizational chart with kings positioned on the top like a CEO, even though kings and queens were generally entombed near the base and centre of pyramids. Or management textbooks will fit the achievements of Egyptian society into modern language: writing statements like 'The Egyptian pyramids are proof that from earliest times civilizations have sought to plan, organize, direct and control work' – even though such civilizations did not express what they were doing in such terms. This approach to understanding life backwards, in terms of the norms of the present day, limits the likelihood of thinking differently.

Mary Parker Follett: The (long-lost) mother of management

Perhaps it is no surprise that the figures identified as foundational in management in the middle of the twentieth century were men. In a male-dominated era, they were a fine council for a field seeking to be taken seriously: Taylor the father of management, was joined by Smith the father of economics, and Weber the father of sociology. But, for more enlightened or modern thinkers, the fact that management appeared to be a motherless pursuit concerned an increasing number of people. If management did not have a mother, then it would have to invent one.

Mary Parker Follett was not invented as much as she was resurrected. Born in 1868, she was a well-known and highly regarded writer and social activist in the early decades of the twentieth century. Then she was forgotten. Subsequently, no young academics in schools of economics or sociology sought to stand on her shoulders. Furthermore, Follett destroyed most of her papers when she became ill in 1929 and a friend destroyed most of the rest after she died in 1933 (Tonn, 2003). Her legacy faded.

Influential management thinker Peter Drucker (1995) tells a story that when he first became interested in management in the 1940s he was given a list of 'key works' to guide him from mentor Harry Hopf. The list was seven pages long and included 'everything of the slightest importance' (Drucker, 1995: 2) but nothing of Follett's was on it. Drucker only became aware of Follett's work when relating his own ideas to pioneering British management historian Lyndall Urwick. Urwick, who had struck up a friendship with Follett in the 1920s, told Drucker the ideas he was expounding sounded a lot like Mary Follett's. Drucker replied, 'Mary who?'

In fact, if it wasn't for Urwick, it would have been hard for later management thinkers like Drucker to recover Follett's ideas. In a world that thought only men were likely to know anything about management, Urwick went out of his way to record and promote her work.

While Follett published two important books, *The New State* (1918) and *Creative Experience* (1924), it was Urwick, with H.C. Metcalf, who gathered together Follett's later papers and speeches, which were often aimed at managers or management associations, and compiled them in *Dynamic Administration: The Collected Papers of Mary Parker Follett* (1940/2004). This is now claimed to be the first management book by a woman (Clegg et al., 2019: 438), albeit compiled by two men.

The title *Dynamic Administration* is a good synopsis of Follett's contribution to management theory. The view of management emerging out of the factories under the banner of scientific management saw organizations as rigid and top-down, where managers issued plans for workers to follow and then sought to direct, control and improve performance according to the 'one best way'. Follett, from a social work and community organization background, saw good organization as a group activity involving the exchange of often conflicting views, from management to workers, workers to workers and workers to management, with the aim of dynamically achieving the best integration of ideas and unifying behind them.

This led Follett, unlike most of her contemporaries, to see conflict as healthy, not something to be managed out or supressed. In 1925 she delivered a lecture entitled 'Constructive Conflict' where she wrote about how good ideas emerged from examining and debating discordant points of view. The best approach to conflict was not to ascertain which side was right, but to seek to understand each perspective and integrate legitimate interests to create new solutions. She sounds very modern as we read her now in phrases such as 'We must face life as it is and understand that diversity is its most essential feature' (Follett, 1924: 300). Diversity and conflict were, for her, the keys to creativity and progress.

In developing her ideas, Follett added to Weber's writing about the rise of rational-legal authority to create the concept of lateral authority. She articulated what she termed the difference between formal 'power over' (or autocratic power) and 'power with' (a collaborative approach) and promoted democratic workplace principles. Her idea of mutual influence saw the possibility for followers to affect leaders as much as leaders affect followers. She viewed management not as a toolkit but as a process of situational decision making where the best decision for the circumstances was arrived at. She was no believer in the idea of 'one best way'. As such, Follett articulated a non-bureaucratic conception of management, urging leaders to replace hierarchies with empowered group networks charged with developing a common purpose. That sounds a lot like the concept of post-bureaucracy articulated by Heckscher 70 years later.

A number of reasons have been suggested for Follett failing to get her due. First, and most obviously, is the notion that she is undervalued because she is a woman. Clegg et al. (2019: 439) see this as important, claiming that she was: 'More modest than her male colleagues [as] she formulated her ideas in only three principles'. But if you read her work, she does not seem particularly modest, she articulated far more than three principles (although others have reduced her ideas down to three), and a number of men on 'the list' are famous for less than three principles.

Drucker and others dismiss the idea that being a woman explains her lack of notoriety, pointing out that other women rose to prominence in this era. However, she did lack the intellectual connections that might come easier to a man in those days. Follett was not affiliated with a university. She had no higher degree, she did not teach and she had no young acolytes.

But a further reason for the lack of uptake is that Follett's ideas did not fit into the emerging narrative of the foundations of management and they lacked a form that would make them easily classifiable. She was not associated with a single school of thought, as Taylor became with scientific management. Her ideas could not be so easily bent into a convenient crutch for a particular ideology, like Smith or Weber. Her thinking could not be plugged into a simple three- or five-step model or grid of types like later theorists such as Lewin and Maslow and Myers-Briggs (who we discuss in the chapters to follow). She could not easily be filed under a sub-field and thus appear in an additional chapter in management textbooks beyond the management history chapter, unlike Taylor (Human Resource Management), Weber (Organization Design) or Gantt (Project Management). Because Follett's theories were inserted late and were difficult to place as a stepping-stone, they took on a kind of ornamental quality for managers – to be admired but not necessarily used.

In recent years, further attempts have been made to plug Follett back into management's lexicon. Her work can and has been linked to thinking on leadership, diversity and creativity, employee relations, the importance of workplace democracy and organizational design. She is even credited with creating the phrase 'win–win'. Sometimes such reverse engineering does not add a great deal to the state of play. It often takes the form of 'look, we can point to a woman as a forebear!' A little forced and more for show. However, we believe that taken more seriously, Follett's ideas can be an important foundation for future management theorizing.

Conclusion

We have covered four founders of management and their theories in this chapter: Taylor, Smith, Weber and Follett. We have explored how these theorists are typically represented in management textbooks, and we have questioned these assumed foundations. This process, which we will employ again in the chapters to follow, frees us up to rethink and construct new foundations that can enable us to think differently about management.

Critical insights

1. *Scientific management became popular because of concerns about the power of big business on society.*

From studying Frederick Taylor and the emergence of scientific management, we learn that management theory emerged in response to a problem that arose at a particular time and in a particular place. That was
rampant unfettered capitalism in the US and its effect on the environment and the lives of future generations. Seeing the earliest management
theory emerging in tandem with a theory about the sustainable use of
resources might encourage us to re-double our efforts to address some
of the environmental challenges the world faces today.

2. *Adam Smith believed an ethical system should underpin econom-
    ics and management.*

Studying the development of Adam Smith's thinking shows how an ethical system should precede the development of management theories. For
Smith, this meant an ethics of moral sentiment, whereby humans trust
and care for others because they can imagine themselves in the other
person's shoes. This created the environment in which a theory that promoted an increasing division of labour can advance a greater good.

3. *Weber did not believe bureaucracy was the ideal organizational form.*

Weber teaches us that organizational forms follow culture. His theory
was not that bureaucracy is best, but that bureaucracy, rational-legal
authority and hierarchical chains of command were the best fit for the
Protestant work ethic that emerged in Northern Europe and the US in
the nineteenth and early twentieth century. We can develop management
theory by exploring different cultures and thinking seriously about the
different kinds of organization that they might support.

4. *Follett teaches us that organizations are unique, and we should
    understand the diverse perspectives within them.*

Follett's thinking encourages us to respect the reasons for the formation
of scientific management rather than its form. Scientific management
emerged in a particular situation in response to a particular problem, so
the style of management that emerged was fit for that particular purpose.
But, once this style of management morphed from that into a 'one best
way', no matter what the situation, it ceased being good management.
Good managers realize that the best decision that emerges from a process will change as situations change. Also, management should be open
to diverse perspectives and the constructive sharing of conflicting ideas.

Search *VSFI Management Theory* in YouTube to watch videos relating
to each critical insight.

3

Management Theory Discovers the Human Worker

> Scientific management ... is widely viewed in a negative light for its dehumanising attitude towards work control. This approach caused a great deal of industrial conflict between management and labour in companies ... it has since been largely replaced by more humanistic concepts of management.
>
> Schermerhorn et al. (2020: 267)

Management studies is a young field, with its origins usually traced to the publication of Frederick Taylor's book on scientific management a little more than a century ago. Taylor's theory was enthusiastically adopted by business owners like Henry Ford. Scientific management and its application in the moving assembly line generated massive efficiencies in production. Some of these efficiency gains were kept as profits, some were passed onto workers through higher wages and some were passed to consumers, in the form of lower prices for mass-produced goods. Cars like Ford's Model T were no longer the preserve of the super-wealthy. Those who laboured to produce them would be able to afford one themselves.

However, those efficiency gains also came at a cost. Scientific management meant managers did all of the thinking about how the work should be done. Jobs were divided up into fragments and workers were required to perform simple, repetitive tasks. Efficiency came at the expense of creative, skilful and fulfilling jobs, with workers becoming a cog in the great machine of capitalist mass production. You might have experienced scientific management yourself, if you've worked in a factory or a call-centre or a fast-food restaurant like McDonald's.

In this chapter, we explore what is considered to be the next 'leap' in management theorizing: the human relations movement and its concern with addressing employee motivation. The conventional account of management's early theories, illustrated by the quotation above, is the story of a transition from the dark days of scientific management, where workers are dehumanized and alienated, to an enlightened period of humanistic management. This is said to have followed the discovery, in a series of experiments conducted at the Hawthorne Factory, that workers have social needs and that managers would do well to understand and respond to these.

This supposedly new realization, sometimes reduced to the phrase 'a happy worker is a productive worker', is an appealing historical narrative for management because it suggests that Taylor got it wrong by assuming that the concept of a productive and empowered employee was a contradiction in terms. As we shall see, the revolutionary discovery at Hawthorne was not so revolutionary after all – and a rather dubious discovery too.

However, the story of human relations theory as a great leap forward took hold, and this prepared the development of motivation theory. Theories which originated in psychology, such as Maslow's hierarchy of needs, were picked up by writers on management and translated for a business audience. In this chapter, we delve into the case of Maslow in detail, because it illustrates how the network of theorists, consultants, professional bodies, textbook authors and publishers, interacted to develop what is probably the most well-known and most misrepresented management theory.

We then describe how this new wave of theorizing had the effect of repressing other explanations of poor motivation, such as Marxist theories. These theorize an irresolvable conflict within capitalism between the owning and working classes. Marxist perspectives, together with theories that focus on how our motivation is influenced by us being constantly watched at work, provide an important counterpoint to managerial theories that dominate best-selling management textbooks and pop-management books.

The 'discovery' at Hawthorne

The story goes that in the early 1920s the Western Electric Company near Chicago wanted to convince its industrial clients that better lighting in factories would result in greater employee productivity. Western's potential clients weren't convinced by the company's sales pitch, so management decided to create an experiment at their Hawthorne plant to back their claims. In this 'illumination experiment' they set up an experimental group (where the level of light was increased) and a control group (where there was no change). As lighting was increased in the experimental group, productivity went up, as had been predicted.

However, output in the control group also went up, which was puzzling. Even more puzzling was that when light was reduced, productivity continued to increase. Clearly, there was something else affecting productivity. But what was it?

The explanation is a theory that has come to be known as 'The Hawthorne Effect' – the behaviour of the workers changed just because someone was taking an interest in them. Those in the control group worked harder because taking part in the study motivated them. While this seems rather intuitive to us today, management's history, as presented in bestselling textbooks, records this as a revelation. After all, we are told, this was an era dominated by a scientific understanding of work, where employees were treated as nothing more than cogs in a machine. Suddenly, there was a recognition that people were not machines after all.

Following the illumination experiment, Professor Elton Mayo from Harvard Business School was called in to do further research. In the 'relay assembly room experiment', six young women, whose job was to assemble telephone relays, were set to work in a room separate from the factory floor. Mayo began to vary the women's conditions of work, first by introducing two five-minute rest breaks. Output went up, so the breaks were increased to ten minutes. Output went up again. Output also increased then the women were given a meal and allowed to finish early. Finally, when all the improvements in their work conditions were removed, productivity went even higher. How could this be explained?

Mayo theorized that participating in the experiment enabled the women to satisfy a range of social needs. Not only did they feel special by taking part in the experiment (the Hawthorne Effect), they had a friendly researcher who discussed the changes with them, rather than being told what to do by their supervisor on the factory floor. They began to identify as a team and begun to socialize together after work. They also challenged themselves by coming up with better ways of assembling the relays.

In understanding the Hawthorne experiments this way, a direct connection can be drawn to theories of motivation. The discovery that a happy worker is a productive worker enabled management studies to pivot away from the scientific obsession with efficiency, to a new field of enquiry: human behaviour in organizations. It challenged scientific management's theory of motivation: that workers are motivated only by money. This is a great story to believe, because it's a win–win. Managing employees in a way that enables them to satisfy their social needs is good for them *and* it's great for the organization. Workers work harder, feel better and get more done.

But was this really a discovery? Typically, management's foundational theories are taught without much reference to the context in which those ideas emerged. In our previous chapter, for example, we showed how the emergence of scientific management as part of the conservation movement has largely been forgotten. The coverage of the Hawthorne experiments can be seen in a similar light. Management textbooks usually cover the experiments that took place within the four walls of the Hawthorne factory in depth, but most say little about what life was like in America at this time.

The sharp deflationary recession of 1919–20 provoked widespread industrial unrest. The final years of the Hawthorne experiments took place during the stock market crash of 1929, which led to wage cuts, increased working hours and work intensification. Threats of dismissal and other exploitative labour practices had become widespread, with unemployment reaching 25 per cent. As we will explore in Chapter 6, there was genuine fear among the business-owning class about the spread of communist beliefs that could undermine the faith in American capitalism.

Professor Mayo and his colleagues at Harvard Business School (HBS) saw these developments as a threat, but also an opportunity. Segments of the population were losing faith in capitalism and business executives, and the business schools like Harvard which produced them were drawing criticism. Faced with adversity, Mayo saw an opening to position HBS as offering solutions to the pressing social and economic problems of the day.

Mayo (1933) believed that what people most fundamentally desired was belongingness, and this was best achieved through co-operative employment relations within capitalism. If workers were unhappy, they should resolve their problems with supervisors. Either by talking through them, or by recognizing that they, or their supervisor, had psychological issues to resolve. The effect of this focus on individual needs, especially belongingness, was to divert attention away from the possibility of more radical change to the way capitalism might operate. Mayo was concerned about the influence of unions, which were agitating for such a change. Mayo criticized unions for only being interested in fighting with management rather than co-operating with them.

Prior to his studies at Hawthorne, Mayo knew that the idea of a happy worker being a productive worker, coming at a time where labour unrest was widespread, appealed to the business community. All he needed was some scientific evidence to back it up. According to William H. Whyte (1956: 35), for Mayo 'the Hawthorne experiments did not reveal so much as confirm'.

In recent decades, others have joined Whyte in suggesting that the Hawthorne experiments weren't a discovery after all. Interviews with those who participated in the experiments suggest that if there was a 'Hawthorne Effect', it wore off after a short time (Wren, 1994). Wren notes that in the relay assembly room test, the workers earned considerably more ($28 to $50 per week) than on the factory floor ($16 per week). They worked harder because they could earn more and for some this was the number one motivation. This was an inconvenient conclusion for Mayo, one that reinforced scientific management's theory that workers are motivated by money, so the economic explanation was downplayed.

Another explanation for the productivity increase focuses on gender – that the experiments involved women, who held a lower social status in organizations at the time, taking orders from men. Acker and Van Houten (1974: 156) argue that 'the females, being weak, had to please the supervisors if they wished to stay in the test room, so they adopted the norm of increased production'.

More recently, Hassard (2012) has filled in more pieces of the Hawthorne puzzle, contesting the idea that Mayo and his team turned Hawthorne around from an authoritarian, bureaucratic organization typical of its time into a more progressive and productive one. By the early 1920s, before Mayo arrived on the scene, it was already a progressive company espousing many human relations- style philosophies. It was also marked by tragedy. In 1915, the company chartered the steamship *SSS Eastland* for its annual picnic for employees and their extended family. Ten minutes after leaving the dock on the Chicago River the ship capsized, resulting in the death of 841 passengers and four crew. The tragedy galvanized the company and its employees, creating a unique set of social bonds among Hawthorne workers.

While doubt has long been cast on Mayo's 'discovery' at Hawthorne, management textbooks have been reluctant to let the facts get in the way of a compelling historical narrative. Perhaps that is because most of us will pay attention to a headline that claims a scientific discovery rather than a small advance or slightly different perspective on what was already known.

Perhaps it is also because the discovery narrative provided much-needed credibility to the field of human relations, or organizational behaviour as it is known today. The Hawthorne experiments created an intellectual space that needed to be filled. If employee productivity was strongly influenced by their levels of motivation, then theories of motivation were required to provide greater insight.

McGregor lays the foundation for more motivation research

Douglas McGregor's theory X and Y, laid out in *The Human Side of Enterprise* (1960), is a useful theory for management textbooks to illustrate the historical disruption in management thinking supposedly brought about by the Hawthorne experiments. Theory X managers, we are told, assume workers are lazy, dislike work and need to be coerced, while Theory Y managers have a more optimistic view of human nature, seeing workers as desiring recognition, responsibility and challenge. The binary of X and Y is a useful one for textbooks: Theory X is the attitude of scientific managers while Theory Y is the attitude of managers enlightened by Mayo's 'discovery' at Hawthorne. McGregor is represented as advocating Theory Y, on the grounds that a more satisfied and committed worker is a more productive worker.

Standard textbook portrayals of X and Y also highlight the limitations of McGregor's thinking: 'Unfortunately there's no evidence to confirm that either set of assumptions is valid or that being a Theory Y manager is the only way to improve employees' (Robbins et al., 2016: 276). This portrayal of McGregor as a poor scientist is a misleading one. As Jacques (2006: 33) notes, McGregor understood the value of scientific knowledge, but he was not the failed empiricist we are led to believe. Far from seeing X and Y as two hypotheses to be tested, McGregor saw them as a tool for getting managers to think about their management style.

The opening pages of *The Human Side of Enterprise* are very clearly about recognizing that all managerial behaviour is based upon a theory or perspective: 'The insistence on being practical really means, "Let's accept *my* theoretical assumptions without argument or test." The common practice of proceeding without explicit examination of assumptions leads, at times, to remarkable inconsistencies in managerial behaviour' (McGregor, 1960: 7). And lest we should misinterpret what McGregor was seeking to do in proposing Theory X and Y, he comes back to this message in the book's final pages: 'The purpose of this volume is not to entice management to choose sides over Theory X or Theory Y. It is, rather, to encourage the realization that theory is important, to urge management to examine its assumptions and make them explicit' (1960: 246).

In modern management textbooks, however, McGregor is typically retrofitted into a narrative of the evolution of organizational knowledge as a science. Remember back to our opening chapter, when we made the point that management textbooks like to highlight their scientific credentials because it helps create the impression among students that management is a serious and worthy subject. It is useful to such a narrative to portray McGregor as supposedly trying to think as a scientist, but not a very good one, and therefore someone we could progress beyond as the field of management continued on to greater heights. This is a convenient narrative, but it is a distortion of McGregor's contribution.

Maslow and other motivation theorists are adopted, and Maslow's hierarchy of needs theory becomes 'Maslow's pyramid'

A similar fate also befell Abraham Maslow. Maslow is probably the most famous theorist in management because his pyramid or triangle of human needs is the field's most famous image. The idea that human needs exist in a hierarchy is typically the first theory of motivation covered in management courses. In our experience, it is the one that students recall most vividly. The theory states that starting with basic, extrinsic needs at the bottom, employees are motivated to satisfy each need level as they progress up the pyramid until they realize their true potential through the gratification of their 'self-actualization'.

What became 'Maslow's pyramid' is a useful point for management textbooks to start their presentation of motivation theories. It is intuitively appealing, and it reinforces a common-sense view of human nature. Students learn that managers should design work, pay and other benefits in a way that allows employees to satisfy their needs, thus leading to increased job satisfaction, commitment and organizational performance. Skilled managers should understand where each of their employees is located on the pyramid and tailor their roles accordingly.

Management textbooks further ingrain the idea of Maslow's pyramid in the minds of readers as they criticize Maslow and his theory. They claim it is simplistic to believe that people are motivated to satisfy just one category of need at a time and that human needs are the same across all individuals and all cultures. They also claim Maslow's theory is unscientific, being based on personal beliefs rather than objective evidence.

These criticisms are useful for textbooks' sequencing, as they describe the evolution of motivation theories from the early, more basic approaches to the more advanced and sophisticated ones. For example, textbooks usually follow Maslow with a discussion of Clayton Alderfer and his ERG theory. Alderfer (1969) reduces Maslow's five need levels to three: existence, relatedness and growth, and does not assume that lower level needs must be satisfied before higher level needs become activated.

Frederick Herzberg (1968) distinguished between 'hygiene' factors, which are extrinsic to the job and include the nature of the work, pay and working conditions, and 'motivator' factors, which are intrinsic to the job and are the higher-level needs in Maslow's pyramid. Herzberg's theory is generally presented as more sophisticated than Maslow's in arguing that attending to hygiene factors can prevent job dissatisfaction, but satisfaction can be increased only by addressing motivator factors.

Supplementing the insights provided by 'needs theories' are 'process theories' of motivation. These concern the decision-making process by which goals are selected and pursued. The two most well-known of these theories are J. Stacy Adams' equity theory (1965), and Victor Vroom's expectancy theory (1964). Equity theory says that we compare our ratio of inputs to outcomes with others. If we believe we are working harder than our comparator for the same pay or working the same, but we are getting paid less, then we will be motivated to reduce the perceived inequality. If we can't change what we get paid, we will reduce what we put in – our effort.

Vroom's theory states that our motivation to work hard towards a goal depends on three judgements:

- What is the likelihood that my effort will result in the task being performed?
- What is the likelihood that my good performance will lead to the desired outcome?
- What is the value I place on those outcomes?

These three aspects (expectancy, instrumentality, valence) have a multiplier effect, meaning that if any of them are low, then overall motivation will be low.

Say, for example, we make an offer to our class that we will pay £2,000 to the person who finishes with the highest score in the exam. Expectancy will be low if students don't believe there is a realistic chance of them finishing top. Instrumentality will be low if they don't trust us to honour our promise and pay up. And valence will be low if £2000 isn't much to them.

Vroom's theory is a good one for understanding why motivation might be lacking, and a useful one for highlighting what managers can do to foster high expectancy, instrumentality and valence, and thus increase motivation. They need to create a work environment where employees can perform at the desired levels, ensure rewards are delivered when performance is attained and provide rewards that employees value.

To summarize, McGregor, Maslow and the motivation theorists that followed are important foundations for management theory. They give management as a subject a credible history populated with well-known theorists. This history charts a progression from well-intended but simplistic ideas from the past, towards a more sophisticated and complete understanding of the topic today. But as we explore in the following section, the most famous of them, Maslow's hierarchy of needs theory, is presented in management textbooks and applied by managers and consultants in quite different ways from what Maslow himself advocated. Exploring how 'Maslow's pyramid' came to be provides an interesting insight into the politics of management knowledge and how this influences the teaching of management to students today.

Who built Maslow's pyramid?

> This profoundly influential pyramid first saw the world in an academic journal in the United States in 1943, where it was crudely drawn in black and white and surrounded by dense and jargon-rich text. The pyramid was the work of a thirty-five year old Jewish psychologist called Abraham Maslow, who had been looking, since the start of his professional career, for nothing less than the meaning of life. (*The Book of Life*)

The Book of Life, an online book published by philosopher Alain de Botton, reflects the popular view that Maslow created the pyramid of needs. *The Book of Life's* detailed reference to the pyramid 'crudely drawn in black and white' in Maslow's 1943 article is perplexing. For a start, there is no pyramid in Maslow's 1943 article. It is also nowhere to be seen in Maslow's most influential book *Motivation and Personality* (1954, 1970, 1987).

This strange absence prompted us to look deeper – did Maslow build the pyramid that people now remember him by? With our colleague John Ballard, we examined all Maslow's published books and articles that we could identify, as well as his personal diaries. John immersed himself in the Maslow archives at the Center for the History of Psychology at the University of Akron in Ohio, and examined many boxes of papers, letters and memos.

We believe Maslow never presented his work in the form of a pyramid or triangle, as it is almost universally depicted in management texts. So, who did? Maslow was a psychologist, but we had a hunch it might have been someone in management studies who created it, since Maslow did not feature in early psychology textbooks. We thought it could have been Douglas McGregor. He popularized Maslow within management circles in his 1960 bestseller *The Human Side of Enterprise*. McGregor introduces the hierarchy of needs in a chapter on Theory X, the set of negative assumptions about human nature which McGregor argues is a traditional but outdated approach to management.

McGregor's description of the hierarchy of needs is striking for two reasons. First, he uses very similar phrasing to Maslow. For example,

McGregor's 'man is a wanting animal' (1960: 36) closely resembles Maslow's 'man is a perpetually wanting animal' (1943: 370). McGregor's 'Man lives by bread alone, when there is no bread' (1960: 36) copies Maslow's 'It is quite true that man lives by bread alone – when there is no bread' (1943: 375). The second striking feature of McGregor's interpretation of Maslow is that it contains many of the misrepresentations of Maslow which feature in management textbooks. For example, when the pyramid appears in management textbooks, the third level of needs is often labelled 'social', but Maslow did not use this term. He called this need level 'love' in his 1943 paper and added 'belongingness' in later publications. McGregor uses 'social'.

Further evidence of McGregor's influence on the interpretation of Maslow's theory surrounds one of the most popular criticisms of the hierarchy of needs – the simplistic view that people are motivated to satisfy only one need at the time, that needs must be fully satisfied before they move to a higher-level need, and therefore that a satisfied need is no longer a motivator of behaviour. As McGregor (1960: 39) summarizes: 'The man whose lower-level needs are satisfied is not motivated to satisfy *those* needs. For practical purposes they exist no longer.'

But if we look at what Maslow actually wrote, he is very clear that while this is one possible interpretation of his theory, it would be a 'false impression' (1943: 388). In explaining his need categories, he is clear that the examples he uses are extreme. For instance, while he says a starving man will be overwhelmed by the physiological need to satisfy his hunger, he is quick to point out that such situations are rare in a peaceful society: 'In actual fact, most members of our society who are normal, are partially satisfied in all their basic needs and partially unsatisfied in all their basic needs at the same time' (1943: 388).

Therefore, contrary to McGregor's interpretation, which is reproduced in many textbooks, Maslow is clear that 'any behaviour tends to be determined by several or *all* of the basic needs simultaneously rather than by only one of them' (1943: 390). To illustrate his point, he offers the example of a person who is satisfied 85 per cent physiological, 70 per cent safety, 50 per cent love, 40 per cent self-esteem and 10 per cent self-actualization.

Another common critique of Maslow today relates to the pyramid's universalizing assumption that all individuals in all societies have the same needs and that these are pursued in the same order. However, once again, although this assumption is promoted by McGregor's use of Maslow's ideas, it was rejected by Maslow himself. Maslow (1943: 387) acknowledged that while most of his clinical patients seemed to have their needs arranged in his hierarchy, there were many exceptions. For some, self-esteem was more important than love. The most important exception was the 'martyrs', who are prepared to sacrifice lower-level needs in the pursuit of self-actualization. Maslow (1943: 390) was clear that 'no claim is made that [self-actualization] is ultimate or universal for all cultures'.

If McGregor's reconstruction of the hierarchy of needs theory is indeed the origin of its representation in management textbooks, it is not surprising that the theory has attracted the criticism it has. The critique is in many respects a critique of McGregor's interpretation of Maslow, without acknowledging McGregor's role as the conduit. However, no triangles or pyramids appear in McGregor's writing, so our search continued.

The first triangular representation of the theory was in Keith Davis's popular early textbook *Human Relations in Business* (1957; Figure 3.1). This is not an equilateral triangle as the pyramid will become, but a series of steps in a right-angled triangle leading to a peak.

Although Davis did not invent the pyramid that textbooks use to illustrate Maslow's hierarchy of needs today, it appears his stepped

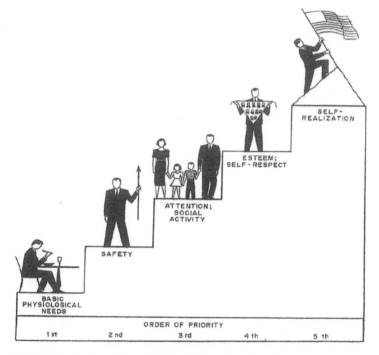

Figure 3.1   Early rendition of Maslow's hierarchy of needs

(Source: *Human Relations in Business*, Davis, 1957, p. 41)

diagram was the inspiration for the first rendition of 'Maslow's pyramid'. This can be found in Charles McDermid's article: 'How money motivates men', published in *Business Horizons* in 1960 (Figure 3.2).

McDermid was a consulting psychologist for the firm Humber, Mundie and McClary. His article questioned what he saw as an over-emphasis on money as a motivator of employees. McDermid arranged Maslow's hierarchy of needs as a pyramid to make the point that once physiological needs were met, managers should focus less on wage increases and more on job conditions which enabled employees to satisfy higher-level needs. By doing this, organizations could achieve 'maximum motivation at lowest cost' (1960: 98). While McDermid did not cite Davis in any way, that he does not use 'self-actualization' (the term used by Maslow) or McGregor's 'self-fulfilment', but 'self-realization' (the term that Davis had substituted), indicates that Davis's particular interpretation influenced McDermid's construction.

The story of who built Maslow's pyramid has a significance that extends beyond the hierarchy of needs theory itself. It is another example of management theories that appear in best-selling textbooks being transformed into something quite different from what they started out being. In the next section, we draw on the genealogical approach developed by critical historian Michel Foucault that we introduced in Chapter 1. This approach explores webs of connection between members of a network that constructs certain 'truths' – in this case, the truth of 'Maslow's pyramid'.

Figure 3.2 Probably the earliest published rendition of 'Maslow's pyramid'

(Source: *How Money Motivates Men*, McDermid, 1960)

▬▬ An analysis of how popular management theories of motivation, like Maslow's pyramid, have come to pass

1. Management academics' need for relevance

Keith Davis, who created the first triangular representation of Maslow's theory, was active in the professional association of management scholars, the Academy of Management, in the late 1950s. He became its President in 1964 and was at the forefront of discussions about the field's emerging status as a profession. To elevate management's status within the university, Davis (1957) argued that management needed to take the teaching of its history more seriously. And to be respected outside the university, management academics needed to position themselves as experts.

The symbol that Davis created out of the hierarchy of needs addressed these issues: the triangle with steps captured the thinking of an important figure in the history of an established discipline (psychology) of which management could claim to be a new branch. Additionally, it gave those sharing their expertise with companies an easy to apply model (we shall come back to this shortly). Davis's addition of the specifically business-attired white executive encouraged the theory's importation into the corporate world of the 1950s and 1960s. It was clearly pitched for the American market too. The flag-raising is reminiscent of the famous image of the flag-raising on Iwo Jima (Cooke and Mills, 2008). It apes what we today might call a meme.

2. Management studies' need for a scientific body of knowledge

Maslow was not a management scholar or a consultant, and his hierarchy of needs theory did not result from an interest in understanding motivation at work. At the start of the 1940s Maslow was watching the world go to war for the second time in 30 years. He believed his field of psychology could contribute an understanding of its causes. After his hierarchy of needs theory was popularized by McGregor in 1960, researchers became interested in subjecting the theory to scientific testing. Maslow did not want to be involved – he was a staunch critic of psychology's obsession with testing theories, which he felt stifled creativity.

But this was a time when the recommendations of two important studies on the future of management research and education, prompted by mass expansion in US business education and the perceived threat to academic standards, were still fresh. A report from the Carnegie Foundation argued that to be taken seriously business schools needed to develop a systematic body of knowledge (Gordon and Howell, 1959).

Likewise, a report from The Ford Foundation identified the need for high-quality scientific research (Pierson, 1959). The foundation defined quality narrowly as being quantitative (based on numbers and facts) rather than qualitative (based on words and interpretations) and it did not want research that raised awkward questions about the desirability of capitalism.

Maslow's hierarchy of needs provided what looked like a testable scientific theory in management studies at a time when there were few to be found. Pioneering organizational behaviour scholars like Clayton Alderfer, who developed the ERG theory we described earlier, wrote of his intense excitement when he read the first edition of Maslow's book *Motivation and Personality*, 'as if a new light had been turned on to illuminate human motivation' (1989: 358). Those, like Alderfer, who put the theory to the test throughout the 1960s and 1970s, greatly appreciated Maslow's stepping-stone towards a new field of research. Maslow had theorized that behaviour was not just the result of unconscious desires, as psychoanalysts conceived, or shaped by rewards and reinforcement, as behaviourists had imagined, but was also driven by the desire to fulfil internal needs.

By the late-1970s, however, management researchers were starting to lose faith in the hierarchy of needs. Wahba and Bridwell's (1976) meta-analysis of 10 studies investigated the theory's empirical validity and concluded it was not testable because of Maslow's lack of rigour, loose language and vagueness in conceptualizing his ideas. However, by the time these criticisms started to gather momentum, another vehicle for promoting Maslow's pyramid had emerged: the modern management textbook.

3.   The emergence of modern textbooks

Most of today's best-selling management textbooks were first published in the late 1970s and early 1980s. These textbooks divided the field into topics, including motivation, and theories were presented chronologically, to show the progression of each sub-field. Each chapter included exercises or cases studies where students could test their knowledge by applying the theories and frameworks. Diagrams, particularly ones divided into steps like Maslow's pyramid, made the subject look practically applicable and made the knowledge easily testable too.

In the age of teaching with PowerPoint, Maslow's pyramid became a staple in slide packs (often developed in tandem with increasingly glossy and graphic-rich management textbooks). Students liked it and because of that, so did textbooks authors, teachers and publishers.

The pyramid has gained further power as it has extended beyond management to become part of the modern fabric of life and pop-culture. Searching for Maslow's pyramid reveals dozens of versions and reinterpretations of the form: pyramids that have wifi and even toilet paper (driven by panic buying at the start of the Covid-19 pandemic) as needs more basic than food, water and shelter. There is even a Maslow Hotel in Johannesburg, dedicated to the hierarchy of needs, with its levels of accommodation arranged in pyramid form.

Although the pyramid is ubiquitous today, a ladder was another common way of conveying Maslow's hierarchy of needs until the 1980s. Then the pyramid became dominant. We think a ladder would be a more accurate representation. The ladder counters the most common misrepresentation of the hierarchy of needs – that people occupy only one level at any time. The depiction of the theory as a pyramid, with horizontal lines demarcating the different levels, makes it difficult to imagine that people can be simultaneously striving to satisfy different needs. When one is on a ladder, multiple rungs are occupied by the feet and hands, and other rungs may be leaned on as well.

4.   Corporations' need for ideas to implement

We've seen how Davis and McDermid's triangular depiction of Maslow's hierarchy of needs helped to translate the theory into a form that could more easily be sold by management consultants. Kira Lussier (2019) traces the uptake of Maslow's hierarchy of needs in the 1960s and 1970s by large corporations like General Electric, IBM, AT&T and Texas Instruments.

At Texas Instruments, managers were given a psychological test that evaluated their perception of employees' motives. They then attended training programmes where they learnt to redesign activities to make jobs more fulfilling. For example, cleaning staff were given responsibility for ordering their equipment, designing how best to undertake their tasks and for setting goals and evaluating performance. And they were paid more for taking on these increased responsibilities. As a result, cleanliness went up and turnover fell. The improved performance might have been influenced by the pay rise workers received, but the reports on Texas Instruments' experience concluded that enriching the jobs was the cause of the increase in motivation, and not the extra money. Just as McDermid had argued, Maslow's hierarchy could be used by business to maximize motivation for the lowest cost.

Popular motivation theories repress alternative theories of poor motivation

Earlier in the chapter, we saw how Mayo used his experiments at the Western Electric Company to support his belief in the benefits of co-operation between workers and managers. This also had the effect of diverting attention away from alternative explanations for why organizations were rife with conflict between workers, managers and the owners of business – explanations which question the desirability and viability of the capitalist system itself. Maslow's hierarchy of needs and its uptake by managers operated in a similar way by offering the promise of a pragmatic solution to a pressing problem.

Like the 1920s, the early 1970s were difficult for the US economy. In 1971, President Richard Nixon responded to an increase in inflation by implementing wage and prize freezes and two years later an oil crisis, which caused the price of oil to increase dramatically, tipped the economy into recession. Workers on American production lines weren't doing well, and they weren't happy. Just like in the 1920s, this was fertile ground for a challenge to the capitalist system to take root.

In 1974, Harry Braverman published *Labor and Monopoly Capital*, combining his experience as a blue-collar worker with his interest in Marxism. Marx (1818–1883) analyzed the role that economic interests have in the workplace, within a capitalist system built on two classes: those who owned the means of production (the land, raw materials and machinery to produce goods) and those who only had their labour and were forced to sell it to the capitalist to make a living. Marx argued that there was a fundamental antagonism between the owners of capital and the sellers of labour, because profit was generated by paying workers less than the value they generated for the organization. Marx defined this appropriation of 'surplus value' as exploitation. According to Marxist theory, this was an antagonism that could not be resolved within capitalism, since increased profits meant increased exploitation.

Braverman drew a direct connection between Marx's analysis of capitalism and scientific management, seeing it as a deskilling process driven by capitalist imperatives to cut costs and increase production with the ultimate aim of profit maximization. The effect of scientific management had been to shift control of the labour process from labour to business owners. As we discussed in Chapter 2, prior to scientific management, employees were largely in control of the way work was done and the speed at which it was done. Scientific management, through its separation of conception from execution and the assigning of conception tasks to management, took control of the labour process from employees, with the result being deskilling and alienation – a loss of meaning in work.

Braverman (1974: 87) did not believe the narrative, popular within management textbooks, of Mayo's human relations movement superseding scientific management: 'Taylorism dominates the world of production; the practitioners of "human relations" and "industrial psychology" are the maintenance crew for the human machinery.' Braverman believed that managers used scientific management to organize how the work is done and to select and train the best people to do the work, and then drew on human relations theories to convince workers of the benefits of this way of working and win their co-operation. This maximizes their output and serves the economic interests of the organization.

Since Braverman saw alienation as inherent to capitalism, he believed it could only be resolved through a radical rupture in capitalism, with workers regaining control of the labour process as well as the fruits of their labour. Clearly, this was not an agenda corporate America wanted to promote. Seizing on Maslow's hierarchy of needs enabled them to reduce the concept of alienation to a lack of meaningful work, which could be addressed through redesigning jobs. Emphasizing the motivation of individuals also had the effect of minimizing structural inequalities and discrimination along race and gender lines. So, for example, poor economic outcomes for Black American communities could be explained away as a lack of motivation that job redesign could address and resolve. Lussier (2019) concludes that Maslow's hierarchy of needs was more than just a practical theory of management. It provided valuable ideological support for American capitalism.

Let's conclude our investigation into Maslow's hierarchy of needs by returning to Foucault's critical historical approach. As we have seen, Foucault set out to map the connections of power and influence that supported the formation of knowledge that came be regarded as true. These truths have particular effects, with those in power gaining through their being in control and others losing out.

Presenting the hierarchy of needs as a pyramid suited almost everyone involved:

- Consultants like McDermid who needed a memorable framework to sell to clients.
- Corporations looking for ideas that would increase morale of their workers.
- The Academy of Management who wanted its members to be seen as being relevant to practice.

- Researchers who could propose extensions to the pyramid to address gaps in Maslow's thinking.
- Textbook publishers and authors who needed not just an idea that had practical applications to the 'real world', but the academic credibility that a 'founding father' such as Maslow could provide (and then a progression that could be demonstrated by showing his ideas to be simplistic and outdated).

And, as a side note, it also suited Maslow personally. Maslow lived for 10 years after McDermid's presentation of the pyramid and did not actively seek to correct it. We don't think that's because he regarded the pyramid as an accurate representation of his theory. A more plausible explanation, from our analysis of his personal diaries, is that aspects of his professional life were unravelling. He felt underappreciated in psychology. The major research journals in psychology had been taken over by experimental studies, which depressed Maslow for their lack of creativity and insight. He also had more 'lower level' motivations, suffering periods of ill health and financial difficulties. Key figures in the management community saw him as a guru and rolled out the red carpet. They gave him the love and status he felt he deserved. Furthermore, through speaking engagements and consulting, he could generate additional income. Seen in this light, it is not surprising he was motivated to go with the flow.

Subsequently, though, the biggest losers, we believe, have been management students. The pyramid is a poor representation of Maslow's theory and the preoccupation with the pyramid obscures the context within which the theory was created. By focusing exclusively on the pyramid, we miss other contributions that Maslow's thinking can make. Following the publication of *Motivation and Personality* in 1954, Maslow emerged as one of the few established psychologists to challenge the prevailing conformism of the 1950s. He spoke out on how large organizations and social conformity stifled individual freedom of expression. He saw this freedom as a precondition for the satisfaction of human needs. Maslow was about individual growth and fulfilment. Knowing yourself and reaching your potential. He was not writing a guide for managers and was at times frustrated that the business community treated his theory of human nature as a means to a financial end, rather than the end which he saw: a more enlightened citizenry and society.

It would be useful if students were encouraged to read Maslow's original writing. Students would better understand that motivating employees to be more productive at work was not the end that Maslow desired for the hierarchy of needs. He was concerned with creativity, freedom of expression, personal growth and fulfilment – issues that remain as relevant today in thinking about work, organizations and our lives as they were in Maslow's time.

The dark side of human relations' theories of motivation

The conventional story of the development of motivation theory is one of progress towards a better understanding of employee motivation. It starts with the startling 'discovery' in the Hawthorne experiments that attending to human needs and providing a happy and fulfilling work environment motivates employees to work harder. Motivation theories from McGregor, Maslow and others develop in more detail how managers can solve motivation problems in their organizations. These theories are criticized for being hard to prove scientifically, but this suits the popular textbook narrative of progress from this well-intentioned but ultimately flawed foundation to more the sophisticated and proven theories of today. It is a comforting narrative for undergraduate students soon to embark on careers, but does it really provide the whole story about motivation? A range of theories, largely ignored by the best-selling textbooks, suggest not.

We've discussed one of those already: Braverman's Marxist perspective concluded that the motivation problem is inherent in capitalist organizations and will never be solved because workers are exploited and alienated. He invites us to question whether today's human relations management really cares about employees, seeing it instead as providing ideological cover for oppressive scientific management practices. Next, we return to the work of Foucault, who provides an interesting perspective on motivation in today's organizations.

If you're reading this book as part of a university course, think about what factors affect your motivation:

- It might be that the course is expensive, and you're concerned about getting value for money by working hard.
- It might be that by completing the course successfully and gaining a university degree that you'll be well placed to land a high-paying job to support you and other family members financially.
- Moving up Maslow's hierarchy of needs, you might also be energized by the connections you have made with other students or your course lecturer.
- Maybe the content of the course has got you thinking critically and creatively about what goes on at work.

We have found that McGregor's Theory X and Y provides useful insights into the motivation of students. Remember, McGregor's key insight was that a lack of motivation might be an unintended consequence of assumptions that managers make about employees. We have observed that some lecturers take a rather punitive Theory X approach to their students, assuming them to be lacking in direction and unenthusiastic about university study. These lecturers feel strongly that mandatory attendance at class should be required. McGregor's theory indicates that this is likely to becoming a self-fulfilling prophecy – that assuming students are lazy will produce unmotivated students. Thankfully, McGregor believed that taking a Theory Y approach would also be self-fulfilling. Consequently, we take a Theory Y approach with our teaching, believing that if we can engage students in what we consider to be the fascinating topic of management studies, they will want to attend class and work hard. This all sounds great – the win–win situation promised by mainstream management studies – happy, studious and productive students. But aren't there other factors that affect your motivation, which McGregor's theory misses?

Foucault (1979) made an important contribution to thinking on the operation of power, using a prison design by nineteenth-century philosopher Jeremy Bentham to illustrate his ideas. In Bentham's Panopticon, the prison was designed in such a way that prisoners were not aware of whether, at any point in time, guards were observing them. Foucault argues that over time, the prisoners will internalize the power relationship and will effectively watch over their own conduct. Modern-day applications are speed cameras. Our knowledge that we are potentially being watched (there may or may not be a camera in the box) changes our behaviour.

What relevance does this theory have for understanding the motivation of students? Think about the extent to which your motivation comes from the knowledge that your work will be assessed and given a grade. When we were students, it was certainly a factor. It explained why we studied hard even on those courses that we didn't enjoy. Now we're professors, we're even more aware of the operation of what Foucault termed 'disciplinary power'. On the surface, it might appear that we have enormous autonomy in our jobs – we can largely research and teach what we're interested in, and mostly we can work at a time and place that suits us.

We, like our students, are largely free to self-manage, but are we really free? Almost every aspect of our work is made visible and judged. At the end of course we teach, students are invited to complete a questionnaire that rates our performance. When we go for promotion, we are required to submit these scores for consideration. The university also publishes those scores on the university website, ostensibly to inform students' choices about what courses to take. A more recent development has been the recording of lectures. There are good reasons for this – the recordings mean the classes are available for those who might be sick, have family commitments or are working, and they are a useful revision tool for exams. But they also make our work visible to those not present in the lecture theatre. It is no coincidence that the software which produces the recordings of our classes is called 'Panopto', in honour of Bentham's Panopticon.

Almost every aspect of the time we spend researching is also judged. Our research is assessed to inform government funding decisions and to signal to prospective students which universities are performing well and which are not meeting standards. It is little wonder, then, that we don't experience much close oversight of our work. Our managers don't need to sit in our classes, because the quality of our teaching can be deduced from student evaluations. They don't need to closely monitor whether we are spending our research time wisely – the research assessment exercise, where our portfolios are judged by senior colleagues from other universities and government, will make that judgement on their behalf. The appraisal of our performance is based on metrics.

In many jobs, surveillance is becoming widespread and largely an accepted part of the job. In retail, there are cameras everywhere as well as 'mystery shoppers'. In call centres, it has become standard for calls to be recorded. For restaurants and Air BnBs, customers judge their performance in online reviews.

We don't deny there is a functional side to all of this. Being constantly watched and judged is a strong incentive to produce high-quality work. It is an important source of motivation. But the point is that you're unlikely to find Foucault's theory of disciplinary power in bestselling mainstream textbooks (a notable exception is Roberts, 2017). Exploring the darker side of motivation would disrupt the conventional account of motivation theory as a happy, win–win story where humans have social needs they are motivated to satisfy, and skilled managers can design work and the work environment in a way that enables those needs to be satisfied. We think both perspectives provide valuable insights into motivation at work. Presenting only one side of the story does students and managers a disservice.

Conclusion

In this chapter, we have seen how well-known theories of motivation emerged in response to the desire to unlock higher levels of organizational performance. Looking again at these theories, as well as theories that are typically excluded from textbooks, can generate fresh insights.

Critical insights

5.   *Human relations theories, like scientific management, emerged to address a crisis in capitalism.*

Mayo's experiments, which demonstrated that humans are more productive when their intrinsic needs are met, were heralded as a discovery. An alternative history suggests that this wasn't a revelation and that Mayo massaged the findings to support his pre-existing desire to promote co-operation in the workplace and to suppress the spread of unionism. Just as scientific management became popular in response to a particular problem (the conservation of resources), so too did the human relations movement – in this case labour unrest and a loss of faith in American capitalism. This reinforces the lesson that management theory generally responds to contextual concerns, rather than being developed in a scientific vacuum.

6.   *Motivation theories were translated for a management audience, and meaning was lost in the process.*

The ideas of Maslow and other motivation theorists were cultivated for a management audience, which resulted in some misrepresentation of the original message. This translation was undertaken by management academics needing to demonstrate the practical relevance of their discipline and to conduct scientific research, by consultants looking for ideas to sell, and by textbook authors and publishers looking for suitable content. We suggest that there is value in trying to understand the original works of these theorists before applying these theories in different managerial contexts.

7.   *Marxist analyses argue low motivation is a product of employment relations within capitalism.*

An effect of the development of motivation theory within management studies was to divert attention from explanations that saw the capitalist system as the root cause of low worker motivation. These theories are generally not included in management textbooks. One such explanation was provided by Braverman, who drew on Marxist theory to highlight economically exploitative relations within capitalism and various forms of alienation as being a cause of poor motivation. Management thinkers should be on the lookout for forgotten or underrepresented theories of management – they can provide us with useful alternatives to add to our knowledge.

8. *Bentham's Panopticon highlights that being under surveillance can be a major source of motivation.*

Another theory that tends not to be included in managerialist management textbooks suggests a dark side to motivation, where the drive to work hard comes from the knowledge that we are constantly being watched and judged. Based on Bentham's Panopticon, this theory challenges the popular narrative that today's workers have high levels of empowerment and autonomy. And given the fact that this surveillance, and resistance to it from workers, is increasing, managers might again do well to consider theoretical perspectives like this.

Search *VSFI Management Theory* in YouTube to watch videos relating to each critical insight.

Fitting the Worker to the Organization: Personality, Groups, Teams and Culture

In the opening chapters we explored the development of management as a field of study. We explained the pressures on US business schools in the 1960s to engage in more scientific research to improve their academic standing within universities and to elevate the status of management as a profession. We also wrote about how textbooks seek to establish credibility with their readers by incorporating classic and cutting-edge scientific research. This scientific orientation of management theory fits nicely with what we described in Chapter 1 as the instrumental purpose of the field – to manage employees in a way that makes organizations more productive and profitable.

We've seen that management studies developed by appropriating theories from long-standing disciplines that don't have this purpose, which has often resulted in a twisting and misrepresentation of the 'borrowed' theories. We examined how Weber's theory of bureaucracy, which explained a shift he saw taking place towards a greater emphasis on rules as a source of authority, appeared initially in management textbooks as a 'recipe' or prescription for how managers could create an 'ideal bureaucracy'. Weber was portrayed as an advocate of bureaucracy and his concerns about its downsides went unreported. We've also analyzed how Maslow's hierarchy of needs, which originated from Maslow's desire to prevent war by illustrating that people share more in common then they realize, became a framework that managers could deploy to get more productivity from employees.

This process of developing theory to fit the objectives and ideological preferences of management is a theme we continue to develop in this chapter. Here we explore and challenge the origins of theories from three core topics in organizational behaviour (OB): personality, group dynamics and culture. From a managerial perspective, *understanding* the behaviour of people in organizations is essential for becoming a good manager. But from this perspective, theory should also help managers to *control* behaviour in their organizations. As one popular management textbook states:

> The goals of OB are to explain, predict and influence behaviour. Managers need to be able to explain why employees engage in some behaviours rather than others, predict how employees will respond to various actions and decisions and influence how employees behave. (Robbins et al., 2016: 212)

Management textbooks used to make 'control' one of the four essential functions of management, alongside planning, leading and organizing. Today, management texts tend not to use the word 'control', probably because it now has a rather negative connotation, related to forcing someone to act in a particular way, even if they do not want to. The word 'influence' is preferred, but the goal, we suggest, remains the same.

In this chapter, we explore well-known theories of personality, group dynamics and culture that appear routinely in management textbooks. As we have done in the earlier chapters, we show the typical portrayal of these theories to be often inaccurate or one-sided. We also delve into some alternative explanations of personality, group dynamics and culture that don't tend to get covered in best-selling textbooks. These theories highlight the dark side of management's control of employees. Matching personalities to jobs, striving to create harmonious and cohesive teams and strong organizational cultures around a shared vision has a dark side of stifling critical thinking, innovation and creativity.

Theories of personality and personality testing: The case of Myers-Briggs

There are two reasons why an understanding of personality can help managers to be more effective. First and foremost, is the matching of people to jobs. Personality tests have become a critical component of recruitment processes, because it is believed that certain types of personality are suited to certain types of job. Get the match right and you'll have happier and more productive employees. Get the match wrong and you'll have unhappy, ineffective workers and an unhappy manager as well. Second, an understanding of personality provides managers with better insight into their employees. Personality, it is believed, can explain why some people are uncomfortable in new situations or find it difficult to make decisions quickly.

The writing of Carl Jung (1875–1961) has been highly influential in shaping understanding of personality. Jung identified a set of dimensions that explained different personalities. Before we look at what management thinking has borrowed from Jung, it is worth noting that our field has been rather selective in what it has taken from his extensive body of work – those parts that cannot be easily translated into simple prescriptions have been forgotten (O'Doherty and Vachhani, 2017).

Jung (1923) theorized that we are split between two worlds. There is an inner, 'unconscious world' that we can only gain access to at certain times, such as when we dream. We also participate in an outer world, the rational everyday world. Jung believed it was important for people to explore both realms of their personality. Two terms that Jung used which you'll probably be familiar with are extraverts and introverts. For Jung, introverts are more in tune with their unconscious world, whereas extraverts are preoccupied with the outer world and reluctant to delve into their unconscious realm.

You might not know that Jung came up with the concepts of extraverts and introverts because best-selling management textbooks rarely mention him directly. Most likely, you were introduced to them as part of the Myers-Briggs Type Indicator (MBTI), a tool for measuring personality based on Jung's theory developed by two of his biggest fans (or 'groupies' by some accounts!).

The MBTI, which gets extensive coverage in management textbooks, identifies 16 different personality types based on the responses to 93 questions. These types are derived from four dimensions of personality proposed by Jung:

- Extraversion (E) versus introversion (I)
- Sensing (S) versus intuition (N)
- Thinking (T) versus feeling (F)
- Judging (J) versus perceiving (P)

Each dimension is regarded as dichotomous, so you are either an extravert or an introvert. Your answers to the questions produce a four-letter acronym which indicates your personality type. ENTJs, for example, are said to be outgoing and decisive and well suited to leadership roles, while INFPs are loyal and enthusiastic about understanding people. The MBTI is very clear that type doesn't change – we are born with a particular personality type.

The MBTI is an indicator rather than a test, in that there are no right or wrong answers. An ENFJ is not better than an INFP, they are just different. As Emre (2019) points out in her book detailing the history of the MBTI, it broke from the tradition of psychological testing being focused on identifying those who were normal from those who were neurotic, psychotic or sociopathic.

The MBTI was created by Katherine Cook Briggs and her daughter Isabel Briggs Myers in the 1940s. Katherine was not a trained researcher, but was fascinated with the concept of personality and had started to develop her own categories based on observations of her family, friends and famous people. Katherine believed it could hold the key for helping people choose work that was best suited to their personalities, which would enable them to reach their full potential. She then came across Jung's (1923) book *Psychological Types*, which had been written off by behaviourists as having nothing of merit for the scientific study of personality. Drawing on aspects of Jung's theorizing, Katherine and Isabel developed their MBTI.

Neither Katherine nor Isabel had any background in psychiatry or psychology, but they were visionaries in seeing the commercial potential of a tool that could sort people into categories and manage them accordingly. The MBTI has become more than just a product – it has become an industry. Each year, more than 2.5 million individuals take the assessment – you might well have taken it yourself. There are certified trainers and coaches, and it has become a regular part of the human resource manager's toolkit.

What the theory behind MBTI lacks is any scientific support. According to psychologist Adam Grant (2013), the MBTI fails all major criteria of high- quality science: reliability, validity, independence and comprehensiveness. A good test is reliable if it produces consistent results over time. When Grant first took the test, he came out as an INTJ, but a few months later when he retook it, he was an ESFP. (Remember, the MBTI assumes that type doesn't change.)

A test is valid if a predicts outcomes, but the MBTI fails here as well. While there is some evidence that people with different personality types are attracted to occupations that suit them, there is no strong evidence that types affect job performance or team effectiveness. Grant is also critical of the MBTI's grouping of certain preferences as dichotomies. For example, it treats thinking as the opposite of feeling, despite a mountain of evidence that thinking and feeling are often 'both' rather than 'either/or', and people with stronger thinking skills are also better at dealing with emotions. Finally, the MBTI is not comprehensive. It's like receiving a physical examination that ignores some of your body parts. It misses whether people have a tendency to stay calm in high-pressure situations and is also silent on conscientiousness, both of which are now regarded as key components of personality.

The MBTI is a useful illustration of a theme we discussed earlier. Management textbooks like to promote themselves as presenting the best science for managers, yet, in practice, many devote multiple pages to a commercial product that lacks scientific credibility. Defenders of the

MBTI argue that its widespread usage is proof of its relevance and usefulness. Opponents would likely point out that horoscopes have broad appeal also, but that does not mean they should be an essential feature of management education or practice.

It would be unfair, however, to conclude that the MBTI is nothing more than a marketing success story. It appeals because it promises to reveal our 'true self' or essence – that all of us are born with a set of preferences that can be encapsulated by four simple letters. It can provide comforting answers to that otherwise potentially endless search to discover who we 'really' are. It doesn't pass judgement on us, and it's easily discovered by answering some simple questions. Who am I? I am an INTJ.

Theories of personality that do better on scientific measures are those that focus on traits rather than types, such as the Big Five personality traits:

- extraversion
- neuroticism
- agreeableness
- conscientiousness
- openness to experience.

In contrast to the MBTI, which sees personality dimensions as either/or, these traits are seen as existing on a spectrum. So, rather than you being an introvert or an extravert, you might be extremely high or extremely low on extraversion, or anywhere in between. Where the MBTI assumes that type never changes (implying our personality is something we are born with), trait theories such as the Big Five acknowledge a mixture of both nature (what we inherit from our parents) and nurture (our experiences, especially in childhood).

Much research has shown that the Big Five traits have high reliability and can predict a variety of outcomes, including job performance and team effectiveness. Perhaps one of the reasons the Big Five has failed to match the commercial application of the MBTI is that few people would enjoy being labelled disagreeable or neurotic or not open to new experiences.

Thinking critically about personality: Theories of identity and the self

The Big Five traits and the MBTI are a good fit with a managerial perspective because they offer the promise of using knowledge of people's personality for financial gain. As we discussed at the start of the chapter, managers are presented with theories that not just explain behaviour, but enable predictions to be made, and therefore employees to be controllable – so that their efforts can be directed in ways that serve the organization's financial interests. This managerial perspective has been challenged by those who are sceptical about the objectives and means of studying personality and want to question the desirability of categorizing people in a way that facilitates their control.

Both the MBTI and the Big Five theories offer the prospect of us being able to discover our 'true self'. That might strike you as uncontroversial, because at some time in your life you've probably received advice from family or friends to 'just be yourself'. Being ourselves means not copying others or caring what they think of us. The assumption underpinning 'just be yourself' is that we are individuals with a true self within us that is waiting to be fully expressed.

According to Roberts (2017), a challenge to this common sense comes from American philosopher George Herbert Mead, who viewed the self as the product of social processes. Mead (1934) believed that we are born with the potential for self-consciousness rather than a developed self. Our early experiences and development are instrumental in the construction of self. We understand who we are by making sense of how others respond to us. For Mead, the self was a continuous and endless process. As our self develops, we create both a sense of who we are, but also what we must be in order to be loved and valued. Early influencers on this are our parents or caregivers. They praise and criticize us, which gives us cues for who we should be, in order to be accepted and recognized. But even after we mature into adulthood and start careers, we remain in this never-ending state of 'becoming', and our work colleagues and managers become important influences.

This account of the self (or what we might describe as our 'identity') being fluid and never complete is different from that offered by the science of personality. While theories such as the Big Five accept that the social contexts in which we grow up shape our personalities, they regard personality as quite stable, especially once we reach adulthood and embark on work careers.

Another difference is that the science of personality emphasizes the atomized or separate individual. Even those theories that acknowledge that our personalities are not fixed at birth but develop during our childhood experiences, see us first and foremost as individuals with particular personality types or traits. In contrast, theories of the self and identity reject the possibility of 'just being yourself', in the sense of being an individual, because our self is inseparable from others – it is constructed and developed through our interaction with others.

This theory of identity and the self can be utilized to explore a dark side to motivation that is generally absent from best-selling management textbooks. We introduced this at the end of Chapter 3 with the discussion of Bentham's Panopticon, the prison design where inmates knew that at any time their behaviour could be observed. We suggested that our knowledge that we are potentially being watched and judged is an important, but often not talked about, source of motivation.

In Chapter 3 we asked you to think about the factors that affect your motivation to work hard at university. In addition to the ones we identified, we could add one more. It might be that you're always comparing yourself to others and that performing well makes you feel good about yourself. You might feel you have something to prove to yourself, and to other important people in your life, such as close family members. Walker and Caprar (2019) believe we live in a society obsessed with performance: whether it's at school or university, at work, on the sports field or in other aspects of our lives. For many of us, performance is a major part of our identity. Sometimes this is positive – defining yourself as a high performer can boost confidence and self-esteem – but there's also a negative side. High achievers can put enormous pressure on themselves to be successful, resulting in stress-based illnesses. They might struggle to take pleasure in their success, seeing high performance as a minimum standard that they expect, but not a cause for celebration. And anxiety about performance might manifest in the form of 'imposter syndrome', in which people, often highly successful people, doubt their accomplishments and live in fear of being exposed as a fraud.

There is evidence that these are exactly the kind of people most sought after by professional services firms – organizations that employ lawyers, accountants, consultants and other highly trained experts. Many students graduating from business schools consider these organizations to be their dream employer. Empson (2018) has spent 25 years conducting academic research into professional services organizations, interviewing more than 500 employees in 16 different countries. She says elite professional organizations deliberately set out to identify and recruit what she calls 'insecure over-achievers'. They are exceptionally capable and highly ambitious but their drive to succeed comes from a profound sense of their own inadequacy. This feeling of never being good enough typically started in childhood and often from a belief that their parents' love depended on them being a high performer.

We can relate to this because we have felt it ourselves, as students as well as in our work, and we have talked to many students who report similar experiences. We live in a society that celebrates high performance, but the flip-side is that organizations can play on our insecurities around performance. If we're feeling insecure, then being seen as a high-performing student or employee offers the prospect that we'll feel better about ourselves. It motivates us.

There is little acknowledgement of this in management textbooks. The conventional story is that if we're happy and have our social needs met, then we will perform well. And also that employees are happiest when they are empowered and given high levels of autonomy. The alternative theory described in this section challenges that happy story and the complacency that it may breed, raising the possibility that organizations get their employees to work harder by playing on their insecurities and by watching and judging their every move. We might feel like nobody is telling us what to do, but we are anything but autonomous and empowered.

Theories of group dynamics and the rise of 'teamwork'

If you have ever applied for a job and read the list of attributes required of the successful applicant, it's likely that being 'a team player' would have been high on that list. Being skilled at working with others in teams is increasingly being held up as important in the workplace because it is seen to provide benefits for employees and for organizations. Teams bring together people with different skills, expertise and experiences, which can mean they can perform better than if the individuals were working alone. This is reflected in the concept of *synergy*, which is where the team effort is greater than the sum of the effort of each individual. Communication technology means that it is easier than ever before to communicate with others. As more companies take their business to a global level, the best employees for the job might be scattered across different countries. Being able to work effectively in diverse teams across multiple cultures is a skill widely sought by employers.

A name that appears in most textbook chapters on group dynamics is Bruce Tuckman, who developed a stage model theory of group development in 1965. Tuckman distilled existing research on how groups develop into four stages: forming, storming, norming and performing.

In the *forming* stage, members are acquiring basic information about what the group is about and are developing a sense that they are a group. An easy way to think about this is when you start a new course at university. You're meeting the lecturer and other students and getting a sense of what the course is about.

The *storming* stage is a period of conflict within the group, as informal rules, or 'norms', are established over the allocation of roles to members and what behaviour is acceptable. There is often conflict in the first lecture of a course around whether it is acceptable to turn up late to class. If a student walks in late, the lecturer might stop the lecture and tell the student that they need to arrive on time. Or they might stop talking, look at the late student and wait until they are seated before continuing the class. Both actions would convey a message to the whole class that such behaviour is unacceptable. Watch also for what happens if the lecturer asks a question and nobody responds. If they move on, it can create a norm that not answering is OK, whereas if they stand there and wait, producing an awkward silence, it's more likely to create a more productive norm of a course where lecturer and students interact in class.

The *norming* phase occurs when this period of conflict subsides. If norms become established that are negative for the group's performance, conflict might surface at a later stage. And, finally, in the *performing* stage the group's structure and roles are clear and group energy is channelled into completing the task.

Twelve years after Tuckman's article outlining the four stages, he published a paper with Mary-Ann Jensen (1977) outlining a fifth stage: *adjourning.* This is the 'death' stage of the group's life-cycle, where the focus is on the feelings of members following the completion of the group's task.

Another concept you'll find in management textbooks is *social loafing*, which originated in a set of experiments published by French agricultural engineer Max Ringelmann in 1913. Ringelmann had the participants (all working-age men) pull individually on a rope for five seconds and measured their maximum pulling effort. He then put them into groups of different sizes and found that as group size increased the average force exerted by participants decreased.

Various explanations have been given for why this happens, including there being a 'free-rider' and a 'sucker' effect. You might have experienced this in group assignments at university. Free-riders reduce their effort because they believe that others will work hard to complete the task, so they need not. This is especially prominent when group members share equally in the outcome of the task, irrespective of the effort they contribute as individuals. A fear of free-riding can produce a 'sucker effect', where group members reduce their effort in the expectation of free-riding – they don't want to feel like the 'sucker' who did all the work.

Curiously, there are other interesting studies on social loafing that tend not to be mentioned in management textbooks. Ringelmann's participants were all men, but what if they had been women? Karau and Williams' (1993) review of 78 studies on social loafing found that men were more likely to partake in social loafing than women. Men are more individualistic and competitive, whereas women tend to be more collective-oriented. Women are more friendly, unselfish and concerned with others, meaning they are more likely to view performing well on a group task as important.

In addition to this gender dimension on social loafing, there is also evidence of cultural differences. People from cultures that emphasize the importance of the individual are more likely to engage in social loafing than those from cultures where people's contribution to the collective effort is given primacy (Earley, 1989). Therefore, if one were to replicate Ringelmann's rope- pulling experiment in collectivist cultures, it would be expected that the group pull would be greater than the sum of the individual pulls – the 'synergy' effect that we described earlier.

It is puzzling why textbooks rarely mention these gender and culture differences. Might it be because the best-selling textbooks originate from countries that celebrate the individual? Might it be because most textbooks have been written by men and that management has been, and continues to be, a male-dominated occupation? Perhaps the scientific evidence on social loafing is inconvenient, even for textbooks that market themselves as being 'scientific'?

Theorizing the dangers of conformity

Even in societies that prioritize the individual over the collective, work almost always takes place in groups. The pressure exerted on individuals when they are members of groups has long interested researchers. Two theories that appear in almost every management textbook are Solomon Asch's research on conformity and Irving Janis' work on groupthink.

Like Abraham Maslow, Asch made a name for himself by challenging behaviourism for its over-emphasis on individual behaviour and its belief that subjective experience and social phenomena were beyond scientific inquiry. Asch believed that group behaviour could not be explained fully by the rational behaviour of individuals, and demonstrated this in his studies of conformity, which places individuals in a group situation. He set up an experiment involving lines drawn on a card.

Participants, who had been told that the study was about perceptual judgement, were seated at a table with seven others, who were all accomplices of the experimenter. The group was presented with four vertical lines and asked which two lines were of equal length. In the example in Figure 4.1, it can be easily seen that lines X and B are of

Figure 4.1   Asch's conformity experiment

equal length. However, when the accomplices all gave a clearly incorrect answer, one third of the time participants agreed with the group rather than trust their own judgement.

Asch's (1958) explanation was that those participants conformed to group pressure, despite knowing the answer was wrong. This has important implications for managers, in terms of encouraging members of a team to speak freely and not succumb to peer pressure.

Another famous illustration of the dangers of conformity is *group-think*, a term coined from George Orwell's dystopian novel *Nineteen Eighty-Four* (1949) about the rules of a totalitarian regime. In management textbooks, groupthink is almost always credited to Irving Janis, who published an article entitled 'Groupthink' in 1971 and a book, *Victims of Groupthink*, a year later (Janis, 1972). Groupthink, according to Janis, is when a norm for consensus overrides the realistic appraisal of alternative courses of action. It is grounded in the belief held by group members that a successful group is one which reaches a consensus. Janis drew on the Bay of Pigs controversy (the failed US invasion of Cuba in 1961) and the Japanese attack on Pearl Harbor in 1941 to illustrate his theory. Groupthink, says Janis, has the following characteristics:

- An illusion of invulnerability which creates unfounded optimism and encourages excessive risk taking
- The collective rationalization of evidence to discount warnings that might lead group members to question their assumptions
- A belief in the inherent morality of the group, which inclines group members to ignore ethical considerations

- A stereotyping of outsiders as evil, weak or stupid
- Direct pressure on dissenters to highlight their disloyalty to the group
- Self-censorship by individuals to minimize the importance of any doubts and contrary views they might have
- A shared illusion of unanimity, with silence interpreted as consent
- Self-appointed mindguards, who protect the group from information that might shatter the apparent consensus.

Janis also offers a number of suggestions on how best to manage these symptoms:

- The leader being open to criticism by other members
- Assigning the role of critical evaluator to encourage the airing of objections
- Leaders appearing to be impartial and not stating their own preferences
- Setting up independent groups working on the same issue
- Discussing the group's deliberations with others in the organization and reporting back their reactions
- Inviting outside experts to group meetings and encouraging them to challenge any apparent group consensus.

It is easy to see why Janis's groupthink theory is appealing content for management textbooks. The use of famous events like Pearl Harbor provided textbooks with ready-made cases that highlight the importance of the theory. Janis's creation of eight symptoms, although motivated by a desire to assist empirical testing of his hypothesis, were an easily-applied diagnostic framework for managers that fitted well with textbooks' preference for a managerial perspective.

But the testing of Janis's hypothesis subsequently proved disappointing. Numerous studies have failed to show a positive relationship with Janis's eight symptoms. Despite this, just as with Maslow's hierarchy of needs, almost all management textbooks include it in their chapters on group dynamics.

What makes Janis's inclusion even more interesting is that he was not the originator of the concept. That honour goes to William H. Whyte, a journalist for *Fortune* magazine who published an article titled 'Groupthink' in 1952. Whyte is a well-known writer – his 1956 book *The Organization Man* critiqued the role of large corporations in American society. It sold more than 2 million copies and is considered one of the most influential books on organizations ever written.

Why does management studies not recognize Whyte as the founder of groupthink? We can't be certain, but by looking more closely at Whyte's work, we suspect it has something to do with his strong criticism of how the field of human relations was developing at the time.

You might remember Whyte from Chapter 3 as one of those who challenged Mayo's so-called discovery at the Western Electric Company. Whyte acknowledged that Elton Mayo had made a valuable contribution to management by bringing the human dimension to the fore at a time when the mechanistic worldview of scientific management was dominant. However, he felt Mayo's pushing of 'belongingness' as the key missing ingredient in the workplace was coming at the expense of the individual.

Whyte did not believe the scientific evidence which claimed to have proven that the group was a superior unit to the individual. If you analyzed problems in organizations only through the lens of group dynamics, he said, you would diagnose it as disharmony within the group and would probably miss the real cause. For Whyte, human relations had become a moral crusade rather than a scientific endeavour. Whyte saw universities as complicit in this indoctrination process, with their emphasis on vocational training and an associated decline in a critical, intellectual education.

Whyte was concerned about the subsequent rise of work groups and group conformity in organizations, which he felt was crushing individuality. Groups, he believed, were instinctively hostile to individuals that challenged the group view, because of the shared belief that a high-performing group was one where there was consensus. That should not be the overriding goal, since progress tended to come from challenging the dominant, taken-for-granted view.

We think understanding the broader context of Whyte's writing provides a plausible explanation of why he is not credited as the creator of groupthink. Would the academic field of group dynamics want to recognize as one of its key contributors somebody who questioned its very existence? It's more convenient to recognize Janis as the founder, despite this coming 20 years later, especially as Janis's conception, with its eight symptoms and actions to mitigate them was a far better match with the managerial perspective preferred by management textbooks.

Organizational culture: A question of 'fit'

We started the chapter by talking about personality assessments that are commonly used when managers are hiring employees. Does that mean that organizations are genuinely interested about you as an individual – to assesses your suitability for the job, to get an understanding about how you might respond to situations and to get an idea of what your strengths and weaknesses are? Whyte believed that while personality tests purported to be about the individual, they were actually aimed at integrating or subsuming the individual into the group. In *The Organization Man* (1956), he included an appendix 'How to cheat on personality tests'. Were he alive today, it's likely Whyte would be further dismayed by the popularity of 'organizational culture' as a management theory that built upon theories of group dynamics.

The easiest way of understanding culture is to think of it as 'the way we do things around here'. It's a set of shared beliefs that influence how we behave. Within the field of management, the most well-known culture theorist is Ed Schein, whom we introduced in the opening chapter.

Schein (2010: 32) defines organizational culture as 'the basic assumptions and beliefs that are shared by members of an organization, that operate subconsciously and define in a basic "taken for granted" fashion an organization's view of itself and its environment'. The main points to note from Schein's definition are that culture is a collective concept, distinct from an individual-level concept such as perception, and that these beliefs are deeply held and often below the level of consciousness. Often, for example, it's only when we experience a new culture through travel, or start a new job, and encounter different belief systems, that we pause to reflect on our existing beliefs.

One of the most popular ways of visually representing culture is to depict it as an iceberg. Schein described three levels of culture: artefacts, espoused values and basic assumptions. Artefacts are the visual manifestation of cultural values – the part of the iceberg above the waterline. Artefacts include architecture, the way people dress, the food people eat, as well as rituals and traditions.

The challenge of deciphering culture from artefacts is that they can be ambiguous. For example, there has been a recent trend in organizations towards removing office walls to create open-plan layouts. This could be interpreted as reinforcing management's belief in egalitarianism, teamwork and open communication or, alternatively, it could be seen as an extension of surveillance or as a cost-cutting measure.

In real icebergs, seawater is denser than ice which means that they float, with most of their mass below the surface. The tip of an iceberg which is visible above the waterline is usually only about 15 per cent of its mass. The iceberg is an appealing representation of culture because the deeper levels lie below the surface and represent the bulk of culture.

Espoused values are typically the official values of the organization, such as customer care, teamwork and quality. They are often reflected in artefacts such as the mission statement and strategy documents. Below espoused values are basic underlying assumptions, what Schein describes as the essence of culture. These are difficult to change because they are often unconscious and taken for granted.

While the iceberg is a popular representation of Schein's three levels, Schein did not create it and he does not think it is an especially good representation of this theory (Schein, 2015b). The 'frozen' nature of icebergs implies that culture is a solid static state, but in reality, it is dynamic and evolving. Schein is reported to prefer the lily pond as a metaphor because, like culture, it is an ecosystem that is living and constantly changing. And, like culture, what you see above the surface of a lily pond is nurtured from below.

Interest in organizational culture emerged in the late 1970s as a response to the challenges facing the US economy, which was experiencing sluggish economic growth, high inflation and high unemployment. In comparison, the out-performance of the Japanese economy led American consultants and researchers to study what made Japanese organizations more successful. They noted that the Japanese tradition of lifetime employment, where employees joined the firm following the end of their formal education and stayed for the duration of their career, engendered strong feelings of loyalty. Employees were loyal to the organization and the organization was loyal to employees.

The American consultants sought to transplant this emphasis on shared values into American management practice. In 1982, McKinsey consultants Tom Peters and Robert Waterman produced a best-selling book *In Search of Excellence*. Their research led them to theorize that 'excellent' companies had in common a shared set of characteristics:

1. A bias for action: getting things done rather than engaging in endless analysis.
2. Staying close to the customer: understanding and responding to customer preferences.
3. Autonomy and entrepreneurship: breaking the corporation into small companies that think independently and competitively.
4. Productivity through people: creating an awareness among employees that everyone is valuable and will share in the company's success.
5. Hands-on, value driven: executives are in touch with the firm's essential business.
6. Stick to the knitting: the company focuses on its core business.

7. Simple form, lean staff: few management layers and small executive teams.
8. Simultaneous loose-tight properties: a culture where employees are dedicated to company values.

Peters and Waterman attracted criticism in the years following the book's publication when some of their 'excellent' companies, like Wang Laboratories, went out of business. However, many of the book's central themes have endured. The final characteristic, 'simultaneous loose-tight properties', is the crux of culture management. Peters and Waterman argued that in 'excellent' companies, employees are deeply committed to the values of the organization. This deep connection, the close bonds and feelings of loyalty that was observed in Japanese organizations, creates an environment of trust, where employees are empowered to take risks and to innovate. This makes employees *feel* like they are empowered and autonomous, but in reality they are tightly controlled – it's just that the mechanism of control is the cultural fit, rather than autocratic management.

If we return to our discussion of bureaucracy theory in Chapter 2, it's not hard to see why the culture idea was so appealing to corporate boards of directors. Bureaucracy theory was popular in the 1970s but by the start of the 1980s it was seen to create inefficient and inflexible organizations. Hierarchical organizations with multiple layers of middle managers, whose primary job was to oversee the work of others further down the hierarchy, were costly to run. Culture management offered the promise of flatter organizational structures that were still under the control of senior leaders, enabling organizations to respond more nimbly to an intensification of the competitive environment driven by globalization. And it encouraged 'insecure over-achievers' to go above and beyond, never slack off or relax – like the Japanese workers who had first inspired the McKinsey team. Peters and Waterman promised senior leaders that 'having one's cake and eating it too' (1982: 318) could now become a reality.

The loose-tight promise of culture management was seen by Peters and Waterman as the theory's greatest strength. However, for critics, it is the theory's biggest flaw. William H. Whyte's concern that the rise of group working was stifling individuality became even more pertinent with the popularization of organizational culture theory. If organizations only want to hire those who live and breathe the espoused values, what place is there for the sceptics and the non-believers?

Hugh Willmott's 1993 paper addressing this question has become a classic in critical perspectives on culture. Like Whyte, Willmott took inspiration from Orwell's novel *Nineteen Eighty-Four* (1949). In the book, the Party used 'doublethink' as part of its large-scale campaign of propaganda and psychological manipulation of the public. Doublethink is the ability to hold two completely contradictory beliefs at the same time and to believe they are both true.

Willmott contended that doublethink is a feature of organizations. Employees are promised greater autonomy if they submit themselves to the corporate culture. This results in workers believing they have freedom when they do not. Willmott sees culture management as an extension of control over workers. In the past, managers were primarily concerned with how employees behaved at work. This was at its most extreme under scientific management when workers had to perform routine, repetitive tasks. Culture management theories, however, seek to control employees' thoughts, emotions and aspirations. It is no longer sufficient to behave in ways that are productive for the organization – workers should 'believe' in their company and do all they can to further its interests too.

Do Whyte's and Willmott's concerns about totalitarian organizations crushing our individuality remain relevant today? You are much less likely than your parents to have a single career or to work for one organization for decades. Popular concepts such as portfolio careers and the gig economy capture the idea that careers are becoming more fragmented, comprising multiple part-time jobs or a combination of employment, contract work, consulting and other activities. Do we really need to worry about having our hearts and minds captured and controlled by organizations?

It could be argued that the celebration of the gig worker is a form of Orwellian doublespeak – on the one hand, it seems positive and individually liberating and creative (the gig metaphor makes a worker sound like a cool artist). On the other hand, gig workers lack job security and are not in a position of strength to oppose the way things are done in organizations, or to stand up for their rights. We certainly think there is value in looking back to the past to understand where Whyte and, more recently, Willmott were coming from.

Conclusion

This chapter has explored three core areas in which management theory has developed: personality, groups and teams, and organizational culture. The four critical insights below summarize the key points gleaned from exploring the historical development and presentation of management theory in each of these spheres.

Critical insights

9. *The Myers-Briggs personality test appeals to managers and employees but has no scientific credibility.*

Many companies use personality tests when recruiting employees because of the belief that a good personality–job fit results in higher performing and more satisfied employees. The Myers-Briggs Type Indicator is a popular measure that suggests we are born with a particular personality type. It purports to reveal who were 'really are' but has no scientific support. It is a good illustration of how theories with commercial potential can supersede other, more scientifically credible theories.

10. *Theories of the self show how organizations categorize and control employees.*

An alternative perspective understands 'the self' in terms of identity, which is constructed through our relationships with others, evolves throughout our lives and is never complete. Many of us invest a lot of our identity in performance, which is constantly measured through an ever-expanding array of metrics. Insecure over-achievers, who are driven to succeed by a sense of their own inadequacy, are often sought-after employees for organizations.

11. *Management textbooks celebrate teamworking but have forgotten earlier concerns about the loss of individuality, creativity and critical thinking.*

In the 1950s, when group dynamics as a management topic became popular, Whyte highlighted the phenomenon of 'groupthink', where individuals were becoming subservient to group values and where contrary views and ideas were unwelcome. This has been forgotten as management textbooks recognize Janis as the creator of groupthink. Janis's concept, as something that a trained manager can handle, is narrower and more superficial, but a better fit with a managerial perspective.

12. *Understanding culture management as an intensification of control over employees highlights the relevance of past debates about conformity.*

The concept of organizational culture appealed to corporations because shared values are an effective way to control employees. Control is maintained, even increased, at the same time as bureaucracy is reduced and some aspects of the work are handed to employees and labelled 'empowerment'. As with the rise of teams, there are risks arising from excessive conformity.

Search *VSFI Management Theory* in YouTube to watch videos relating to each critical insight.

5

Heroic Leaders and the Glorification of Change

We live in a world obsessed with leaders. In politics, voters appear more interested in leaders than parties and their policies, with elections won and lost on the popularity of the leader's image. In business, chief executives Elon Musk (Tesla), Jeff Bezos (Amazon) and Mark Zuckerberg (Facebook) have become celebrities. While you might think that running companies is a task best performed by rational, thoughtful and serious people, we talk about business leaders in religious tones. What is their vision? What values do they stand for? Can they inspire their followers and lead them to the promised land (of higher profits)?

We often start our classes on leadership by asking students about what they see as the differences between leadership and management. 'Leadership', they generally say, is about having a vision, charisma, inspiration, courage, self-confidence and strength of conviction. In other words, lofty and grand. 'Management' not so much. It is about compliance, process, giving orders and formal authority. We suspect that if we randomly asked people on the street, they would come up with similar answers.

Management textbooks inform and perpetuate this thinking. Schermerhorn et al. (2020: 465) distinguish 'change leadership' from 'status quo management'. Leaders are portrayed in a positive light – being confident, seizing opportunities and making things happen. The corresponding descriptions of managers are negative – they are reluctant to take risks, are bothered by uncertainty and wait for things to happen. Students are taught that leaders promote creativity and innovation (which are assumed to be good), while managers get in the way of these things. Also noteworthy is the way leadership and change are interconnected. Leaders are dynamic people who create change. In contrast, managers can't or won't change.

The origins of this binary view can be traced to an article 'Managers and leaders: Are they different?' by Abraham Zaleznik in *Harvard Business Review* in 1977. Like many articles in this popular business publication, it was an opinion piece based on the author's observations of business, rather than any systematic research. Zaleznik argued that managers and leaders are very different kinds of people, who think and act differently. Leaders bring inspiration, vision and passion to their organizations and drive corporate success. Managers, on the other hand, focus on processes and stability and hold their organizations back.

We conclude our classroom exercise exploring the differences between leadership and management by asking students who they would prefer to be – a leader or a manager? Unsurprisingly, nobody wants to be a manager. They all want to be leaders. It is a curious feature of management as a field of study, that it has evolved to a point where it 'eats itself', denigrating the very occupation that bears its name. 'Come and study in the school of management but whatever you do, don't be a manager!' It would be hard to imagine medical schools telling their students 'don't be a doctor!'. Management has handed over the mantle to a new field: leadership, which has gone from strength to strength (Jackson and Parry, 2018).

In this chapter, we explore how these simplistic portrayals of leaders and managers came to be seen as facts and make an argument for why they are damaging. We show how leadership theory has gone full circle, with theories rejected in the past resurfacing and becoming dominant. What is concerning is that there were good reasons for dismissing these theories, reasons that remain as relevant today as they were then. Appreciating this history of leadership theory enables us to think critically about the state of leadership today, and to see how it might be different. Opening up different understandings of what leadership means offers the promise of fairer, more just, and better organizations.

Natural born leaders

Typically, leadership chapters in management textbooks begin with the theory that leaders are born with a set of genetically-determined characteristics or 'traits' – traits that mirror the list our students come up with in the management versus leadership exercise. As Scott Taylor (2015) notes, it's a bit of a stretch to call the early writers on this approach 'theorists', because what they created were really just biographies. In this 'Great Man' approach (they were almost always written by men about other men), the biographer focused on someone widely regarded to be an important leader, analyzed their life-history and behaviour patterns and then attributed their success to particular personality characteristics.

In the twentieth century, the field of psychology developed further this trait approach. This was appealing to those interested in management because it implied that organizations could identify people who possessed those traits, place them into leadership roles and be confident they would succeed. Trait research was summarized by Stogdill

(1948), who found that factors such as intelligence, originality, initiative and persistence were associated with leadership. However, Stogdill also highlighted a problem with trait theory – it focused exclusively on understanding leaders and paid no attention to their followers. You've probably heard the phrase 'you're only a leader if someone is following'. If leadership is a relationship between leaders and followers, then it probably would make sense to know something about the followers!

A second problem with trait theory identified by Stogdill was that it paid no attention to the situation or context within which the leader was operating. If we look back through time, we see many examples of leaders who were regarded as being successful in one situation but not in another. US President George W. Bush holds the record for having the highest and lowest presidential job approval rating in the Gallup Poll, which has been surveying US public opinion for more than 80 years. Bush's approval rating surged to 90 per cent in the immediate aftermath of the September 11 terrorist attacks in 2001 when he offered reassurance but also promised a forceful, retaliatory response (Schubert et al., 2002). Bush tended to see issues in 'black and white' terms, an approach that suited the moment. However, when the immediate shock and sense of crisis faded, and the focus of foreign policy became the complex weighing of evidence regarding whether Saddam Hussein was hiding weapons of mass destruction, Bush was less effective. Critics questioned whether he possessed the intellect to make sound judgements and his approval rating in the Gallup Poll fell to a low of 25 per cent.

Failing to account for followers and the situation are two criticisms of trait theory that appear regularly in best-selling textbooks, but there's a third critique that tends not to appear. This criticism may best be explained in reference to the most infamous leader of the twentieth century – Adolf Hitler. If we look back to our characteristics of leaders, it could be argued that Hitler ticked all the boxes – from his vision to make Germany great again to his self-confidence and strength of conviction. Watching Hitler's speeches on YouTube makes it hard to argue that he wasn't compelling, decisive and charismatic: a real leader.

Hitler's rise revealed the dark side of trait theory. The natural born leader can be a force for good, but also a force for evil, so people begun to think twice about whether it was wise to have charismatic visionaries in positions of power.

Theorizing how leaders are 'made'

The ascent of Hitler and other dictators, such as the Soviet Union's Joseph Stalin and Italy's Benito Mussolini, led leadership theorizing in a new direction, based on the premise that successful leaders are 'made' (i.e. trained or educated) rather than born. This approach to leadership sought to identify effective leadership behaviours. The premise was that anybody could be trained to be a leader, regardless of their innate characteristics.

The most well-known behavioural studies were undertaken at the University of Iowa in the late 1930s by Kurt Lewin, a Professor of Child Psychology, his graduate student Ronald Lippitt and another researcher, Ralph White. Lewin was born into a Jewish family in Poland and moved to Germany when he was 15. When Hitler came to power in 1933, Lewin fled Germany and emigrated to the United States, working first at the University of Iowa and then at the Massachusetts Institute of Technology. Management textbooks typically state that Lewin and his associates tested to see which of three leadership styles were most effective: democratic, autocratic or laissez-faire. A democratic leader involves employees in decision making, whereas an autocratic leader does not. The laissez-faire style is defined as giving employees complete freedom.

In fact, the initial studies, of young boys at a club, were set up only to measure the effectiveness of democratic versus autocratic approaches. As Michael Billig notes, Lewin's theory building was shaped by his personal experience of fascism. Unsurprisingly, Lewin hoped the results would prove democratic leadership to be more effective than autocratic leadership. However, in one group of children under the democratic mode, the group descended into anarchy. Negative results for 'democracy' were not the desired outcome, so Lewin created a third category called laissez-faire. 'Thus, Lewin protected the concept of "democracy" rhetorically, attributing the "bad" results to a form of non-democratic leadership' (Billig, 2014: 450).

In any event, Lewin was unable to draw definitive theoretical conclusions about what leadership style was most effective. As we saw with trait theory, it depends on the situation. Democratic leadership often produces higher levels of performance, but not always. In certain situations, autocratic leadership is more effective. In moments of crisis, when people are looking for 'strong leadership' and there is little time to make decisions, having someone take control and commit to a course of action can be well received.

Next came a group of theories that sought to determine what leadership behaviours are effective in various situations – these became known as contingency theories of leadership.

Fred Fiedler's contingency model of leadership, dating from the 1960s, started with a questionnaire that determined whether the leader was relationship oriented (interested in maintaining good personal relations) or task focused (interested in getting the job done). Next came evaluating situations based on an assessment of the strength of the relationship between the leader and followers, the structure of the task and the formal authority held by the leader. Once this analysis was complete, Fiedler claimed it was possible to determine which style of leadership best fitted the situation. His theory suggested that if it wasn't possible to change the leader, it might be possible to change the situation to make it a better fit with the existing leader (Fiedler, 1967).

While contingency theories like Fielder's remain a feature of today's textbooks, we suspect that they don't get the attention they used to. They have fallen out of fashion, replaced by theories about special individuals who can achieve extraordinary results.

The return to heroic leadership

Transformational leadership, probably the best known and most influential leadership theory today, originated with political scientist James MacGregor Burns' book *Leadership* (1978). Burns distinguishes between transactional and transformational leadership. In transactional leadership, 'leaders approach followers with an eye to exchanging one thing for another: jobs for votes, or subsidies for campaign contributions' (1978: 4). In contrast, 'the transforming leader looks for potential motives in followers, seeks to satisfy higher needs, and engages the full person of the follower' (1978: 4). For Burns, it was vital that followers have knowledge of alternative leaders and can choose alternative leaders if they wish; and that leaders take responsibility for delivering what they promise. We'll return to the significance of this insight shortly.

Burns' book appeared at the same time as Zaleznik's article about the differences between leaders and managers. Those like Zaleznik, who believed that the behavioural approach had run its course, needed a new leadership theory to promote. Transformational leadership was a perfect fit and attracted scholars from leading US business schools. Bernard Bass and Ronald Riggio (2006) describe how transformational leaders are able to articulate higher goals which leaders and followers share in common. Through this goal realignment, leaders stimulate and inspire followers, leading to higher levels of performance, satisfaction and commitment to the organization. This offers an appealing win–win situation – for organizations and their leaders, but also for empowered employees.

Transformational leadership theory was also a marketable product for business schools looking to attract students. Harvard Business School created high-priced courses for business executives from around the globe – the pitch was hard to resist: get a qualification from one of the world's best universities and become a heroic, transformational global leader.

The view that managers and employees are working towards shared goals is a recurring theme in best-selling management textbooks. However, it is just one perspective on the relationship between employees and organizations. Alan Fox made an important contribution to thinking about this with his 'frames of reference' theory in the 1960s. Like Douglas McGregor (1960), Fox starts with the insight that while management is typically thought about as a practical activity (as opposed to something theoretical), it is always based on a set of assumptions. Whereas McGregor was interested in assumptions managers make about workers (Theory X or Theory Y), Fox was interested in assumptions managers make about the nature of the employment relationship.

In Fox's *unitarist* frame or paradigm, it is assumed that owners, managers and employees share a common interest in the survival and growth of the organization. Since there is one unified goal, organizations should be co-operative and harmonious. Therefore, where conflict does arise it is seen as dysfunctional – either the result of external groups (such as unions) seeking to interfere unnecessarily in the employment relationship, or incompetent leaders failing to communicate the shared goal. Unitarism also assumes management to be the sole source of legitimate authority and to represent what is best for the organization. We can see the compatibility between a unitarist frame of reference and transformational leadership – leaders articulate shared goals and motivate people to pursue those goals, resulting in higher levels of organizational performance.

Fox (1966) observed that the field of management was dominated by the unitarist frame, but it did not match what he saw as the reality of organizational life. A more realistic perspective, he theorized, was to see organizations as like a plural society comprised of different groups that share some common interests but also can have separate interests and objectives. So, for instance, employees who belonged to unions could have loyalty to their unions as well as loyalty to the organization. Sometimes those loyalties could conflict, such as in pay negotiations, where higher pay for employees could reduce the organization's profits, and vice versa.

Hence, rather than seeing conflict as dysfunctional, *pluralists* regard it as inevitable and normal, to be resolved by organizations involving employees and their unions in decision making. Fox believed it was vital for students to understand both unitarist and pluralist frames. If organizations had divergent interests but managers proceeded on the basis of a shared common purpose, 'team mythology may be not only irrelevant but positively harmful' (Fox, 1966: 374). However, more than 50 years after Fox raised concerns about management education being dominated by unitarist assumptions, not much seems to have changed – in fact, the unitarist perspective may be even further entrenched. It is an entrenchment that can lead to some negative outcomes, as we explore in the next section.

The dark side of transformational leadership theory

Leaders and followers working together to achieve common goals might sound great in practice, but there is an important difference between the political arena, where Burns came up with the concept of transformational leadership, and the business world. Employees usually don't get to vote for who leads them, nor can they vote their leaders out if they break their promises. What, for Burns, was an important mechanism to keep transformational leaders in check was forgotten when his theory was eagerly brought into the field of management by others.

Organization theorist Dennis Tourish (2013) worries about this, pointing out that transformational theory shares much in common with 'cults'. Cults typically have a charismatic leader and a compelling vision. Followers are rewarded for compliance and penalized for dissent. Followers are encouraged to believe the leader has their best interests at heart and a common culture is seen to be necessary for the group to succeed, making dissent or critique even less likely. A tragic illustration of these dynamics occurred in the 1978 Jonestown massacre of 918 members of a cult led by American preacher Jim Jones. Jones founded his Peoples Temple church in the US but following publicity about church members being physically and mentally abused, he relocated to the jungle in Guyana. When an American politician travelled to the settlement to investigate claims that church members were being held against their will, Jones ordered his followers to drink juice laced with cyanide. Those who refused were forced to do so by armed guards.

If we accept there are dangers in transformational leadership, what alternatives are there? Tourish wants us to give serious consideration to Burns' pluralist notion of transactional leadership – the idea of leaders recognizing that followers might have different interests and objectives – and therefore to engage in some 'give and take' around that.

A second alternative is to consider more democratic processes in organizations. Remember, Burns believed that the ability of followers to elect their leaders was a necessary safeguard against the threat of transformational leaders going rogue. What if employees were given the right to choose who leads them, as well as the power to replace them?

Industrial democracy, defined as any system of employee representation that gives workers a say in how companies are run, does not feature much in best-selling US management textbooks. Smith et al. (2019) note that a distinctive feature of American capitalism is the near absence of applications of industrial democracy which are common in European firms. In many German firms, for example, worker representation on company boards is mandatory. This is rare in the US nowadays but, interestingly, between 1910 and 1930 many American firms experimented with systems of worker representation, such as work councils and shop committees, based on their observation of what was happening in other countries. This approach was seen as benefitting organizations by reducing tensions between employees and management by ensuring employee interests and perspectives were heard by management. Efficiency improvements also resulted from employees having an opportunity to make suggestions for how the companies could be run. However, from the 1930s, industrial democracy gradually fell out of favour in the US.

As we've explained above, most management textbooks favour a unitarist perspective. Unitarists might argue that employees usually don't have an ownership stake in the business and would therefore not vote for what is best for it. They might vote in leaders who will give them pay rises or 'go easy' on them. We're not saying that the idea of more democratic structures in organizations isn't complex or problematic. But we do believe the issue warrants more serious consideration, especially in an era where heroic conceptions of leaders dominate.

We turn now to a new twist on transformational leadership theory that has become popular in recent years.

Authentic leadership

Psychologist Adam Grant (2016) believes we live in the 'Age of Authenticity, where "be yourself" is the defining advice in life, love and career'. Just like transformational leadership, the theory of authentic leadership promotes a virtuous circle starting with great leaders who energize followers to produce extraordinary outcomes for organizations, resulting in higher profits. The point of difference with transformational leadership theory is that leaders' 'authenticity', rather than their charisma, is the spark. By being self-aware and acting with integrity, authentic leaders are positive role models for followers (Avolio and Gardner, 2005).

If you follow politics, there's plenty of evidence of the popularity of authentic leadership. It is common for candidates to try to position themselves as 'real people' rather than politicians (attempting to obscure the obvious: that they are competing for political office!). The impression is that 'real people' are honest, genuine and have integrity, whereas politicians are like performers in a stage production – being 'politically correct' in order to secure votes, but not really believing in what they say. Just like management 'ate itself' to promote leadership as better than management, politics similarly eats itself – following authentic leadership theory – perversely suggesting that politicians are bad people. Real people (i.e., non-politicians) are more authentic and therefore better. (But by wearing this mask, as Erving Goffman (1959) might call it, you can argue that 'real-people' politicians are the most disingenuous and inauthentic. There is more on this conundrum to follow.)

Authenticity (or at least the perception of authenticity) was a key to Donald Trump's election as US President in 2016. A feature of Trump's campaign were the personal insults he dished out to anyone who opposed him. In the documentary *Trump's Road to the White House* (2017), his campaign manager Corey Lewandowski recalled the time Trump criticized American war hero and former Republican presidential candidate John McCain in a television interview. Trump said McCain was 'a war hero because he was captured. I like people that weren't captured'. Lewandowski advised Trump to issue an apology, but Trump refused. Lewandowski later reflected that 'Donald Trump understood things that I didn't about the American people. Once I understood that he was prepared to double down on his comments and be a fighter for what he believes in, I'm all in and I'm there with you, to support you.' For the rest of the campaign he decided to 'let Trump be Trump' (*Trump's Road to the White House*, 2017).

Politicians' claims to be authentic doesn't always work out well, however. Former Australian Prime Minister Julia Gillard, in the lead-up to the 2010 election, felt her party's campaign had been overly stage-managed and 'spin-driven', and she wanted more authenticity. So, she went public with the statement 'It's time to make sure the real Julia is well and truly on display' (Gillard, 2014: 46). While her desire for openness resonated with some sections of the Australian media, her critics concluded this meant that she had not been 'real' or 'authentic' in the past.

Just as Hitler was a problem for transformational leadership theory, it can be argued that Trump is a problem for authentic leadership. While many of Trump's supporters value his authenticity, many opponents believe he's a liar and a fraud – which would be regarded by many as the opposite of authenticity.

Psychologist Scott Kaufman (2019) says that from a scientific perspective, research on authenticity is a mess. First, there's a lack of agreement about what it means to be authentic. Are you being authentic when you are being consistent with what you truly believe, whatever those beliefs are? So, say Trump believes in the value of telling lies, does that make him authentic when he's telling lies? As with transformational leadership, advocates of authentic leadership theory only want to be associated with leaders of 'high moral character' (Avolio and Gardner, 2005: 321). That's convenient because it allows them to distance themselves from leaders, who they believe are lacking in morality. But if authenticity is about 'being ourselves', isn't the person of low moral character (however defined) being authentic when they act accordingly?

A second problem with the concept of authenticity relates to our discussion of the self in Chapter 3. The notion that it's possible to 'just be ourselves' is based on an assumption that we are unique individuals, rather than seeing the self as socially constructed through our relationships with others.

A third problem is how to measure authenticity. It's almost always done through self-report measures, such as questionnaires. However, just because someone tells you they are being authentic, are they? How do we really know? Self-reports seem to be a poor method for building theory scientifically, but there is no other obvious way of measuring authenticity.

Even if we could measure it, do we really want our leaders to be authentic? Jeffrey Pfeffer answers that with a resounding 'no', arguing that 'being authentic is pretty much the opposite of what leaders must do' (2015: 87). Rather than being true to themselves, Pffefer believes they must be true to what followers need from them. So, if followers need reassurance, then leaders should offer that and project confidence, even if it means hiding doubts they might be feeling.

Adam Grant (2016) highlights research that suggests being authentic at work does not pay off. Some of us are what psychologists call 'high self-monitors' – we read social situations and try hard to fit in and avoid offending anyone. In short, high self-monitors are less authentic, because they're skilled at monitoring how they come across to others. Low self-monitors, on the other hand, are more authentic, because they are less concerned about what others think of them. Research suggests that high self-monitors tend to receive higher performance evaluations and are more likely to be promoted into leadership positions. In other words, low self-monitors pay a big price for being authentic.

There's also an interesting gender dimension to authenticity. Women are more likely to be low self-monitors. Perhaps, says Grant, because of social pressures to express their feelings. For those in leadership positions, sharing their feelings and insecurities may be interpreted as a sign of weakness, causing others to evaluate women's leadership negatively.

We return to this idea later in the chapter, when we introduce a gender perspective on leadership. But first, we explore the links between leadership and change that we alluded to at the start of this chapter.

Leading change

While leadership research has been around for a century, change management emerged as a major sub-field within management only in the last 40 years. It is now one of the most popular topics, as seen by the growing number of university degree specializations and courses being offered. As we have seen, the concepts of change and leadership are closely connected – the generally promoted (and seen to be 'common-sense') view is that leaders are people who create change.

In most management textbooks, the foundations of change management are traced to Kurt Lewin. Lewin contributes two theories whose influence continues to this day: force-field analysis and 'change as three steps'. In Lewin's force-field theory, organizations exist in a static (otherwise known as equilibrium) state, that is, held in place by two opposing forces. *Driving* forces can be external to the organization, such as changes in the political, economic, social and technological environment. Or they can be internal, such as a change in the organization's strategy. *Restraining* forces are usually thought about in terms of people who resist change (more on that shortly). The force-field theory tells us that to create change in organizations, leaders can increase the driving forces, decrease the restraining forces, or do both.

Lewin's second theory, often referred to as 'change as three steps' (Figure 5.1), builds upon the idea of the force-field. Management textbooks state that since organizations generally settle into an equilibrium state, they need to be 'unfrozen' by leaders before change can be implemented. Once leaders have successfully created the awareness that change is necessary, the implementation phase can then proceed. In order for these changes to become the new 'business as usual', the organization needs to be 'refrozen' – again, under the eye of the leader.

This representation of Lewin's theory makes a series of assumptions about leaders and followers and about the nature of change. In particular, it reinforces the heroic portrayal of leaders as highly skilled,

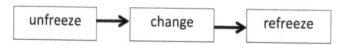

Figure 5.1   A representation of Lewin's 'change as three steps'

powerful people who can change organizations according to their desire. This contrasts with viewing organizations as being shaped by changes in the external environment that tend to be beyond leaders' control. Lewin's change leader is proactive and powerful. The model assumes that change is necessary and in the best interest of the organization. It also implies that lower-level employees cannot see the need for change and are likely to resist it.

Lewin's two foundational ideas, the force-field and 'change as three steps', have informed numerous influential change models. The most famous is John Kotter's eight steps for successfully transforming organizations:

1. Establish a sense of urgency.
2. Form a powerful guiding coalition.
3. Create a vision.
4. Communicate the vision.
5. Empower others to act on the vision.
6. Plan for and create short-term wins.
7. Consolidate improvements and produce still more change.
8. Institutionalize new approaches.

Kotter's eight-step model is promoted as a universal prescription, suitable for any organization, in any industry, in any country. This is central to its appeal and popularity. Kotter claims that if leaders follow the eight steps, they will successfully lead change. The model was published in *Harvard Business Review* in 1995 and reprinted in 2007 because of its continued influence. In 1996, Kotter published *Leading Change* (reprinted in 2012), rated by *TIME* magazine (2014) as one of the 25 most influential management books ever written.

Kotter does not directly acknowledge Lewin's three-step model, but it's easy to spot the similarities. Steps 1–4 involve 'unfreezing', steps 5 and 6 involve 'changing', and the final two steps of consolidation and institutionalization are 'refreezing'. Step 7 is also noteworthy for the statement 'produce still more change'. Once the change has been completed, the leader's task is to create another change – it is assumed that change is good, and more is better.

There's something very curious about the way Lewin's three-step theory is presented in management textbooks. Students are typically informed that:

•   Lewin was a great scientist with a keen interest in management
•   discovering 'change as three steps' was one of his greatest endeavours

- his simplistic approach to managing change has subsequently been built upon.

However, the more that we looked at the origins of 'change as three steps', the more we saw the anomalies between what Lewin actually wrote and how he is represented.

For example, French and Bell's *Organizational Development* (5th edition, 1995: 81) states that Lewin's force-field and 'change as three steps' theories 'have been influential since the 1940s'. However, the earlier editions of their *Organization Development* text (1973–83) make no mention of 'change as three steps'. If these theories had been influential since the 1940s, why weren't they mentioned in the early editions? Our research suggests that prior to the 1980s, the theory wasn't influential at all: probably because it was little more than a passing idea for Lewin.

The fragment that would be developed into the model is from an article published in 1947 entitled 'Frontiers in Group Dynamics': the first article of the very first issue of the journal *Human Relations*. It is buried there in the 24th of 25 sub-sections in a 37-page article. No empirical evidence is provided, or graphical illustration given, and unlike Lewin's other writings, the idea is not well integrated with other elements. It is merely described as a way that 'planned social change may be thought of' (Lewin, 1947: 36); just an example explaining (in an abstract way) the group dynamics of social change and the advantages of group versus individual decision making. It appears almost as an afterthought, or at least as not being fully thought out. Having searched Lewin's publications, written or translated into English (67 articles, book chapters and books), the Lewin archives at the University of Iowa, and the archives at the Tavistock Institute in London where *Human Relations* was based, we can find no other origin for 'change as three steps' apart from these few words published in 1947, the year he died.

Lewin never presented the theory in a linear diagram like we see in Figure 5.1, and he never wrote his idea was a model or theory that could be used by a change agent. He was adamant that group dynamics must not be seen in simplistic terms and believed that groups were never in a steady state, seeing them instead as being in continuous movement, albeit having periods of relative stability or 'quasi-stationary equilibria' (Lewin, 1951: 199).

Furthermore, despite what textbooks lead us to believe, Lewin was not a management theorist – remember, at Iowa he was Professor of Child Psychology. He was, however, involved in one major study of corporate change, at the Harwood Manufacturing Corporation. This study concluded that change was most successful when those affected were meaningfully involved in designing the change, rather than it being determined by those at the top of the organization.

Yet, the three-step model and Kotter's adaptation are highly leader-centric. They convey the idea that it is the leader's responsibility to create the vision and communicate this down the layers of the organization, rather than involve those affected by the change in its development. It is, in the terms of Fox's (1966) frames of reference, unitarist rather than pluralist. We reckon Lewin would be shocked to see how his ideas are represented in textbooks today.

So, why did 'change as three steps', which was largely unknown prior to the 1980s, quickly become the intellectual foundation of the fast-growing field of change management?

Around 1980, a new phenomenon emerged: pop-management. This was fuelled by a growing number of managers eager for knowledge that could help them climb their career ladder. There was also, as we described in Chapter 4, concerns about the relative under-performance of US companies, which turned books like *Theory Z* (Ouchi, 1981), *The Art of Japanese Management* (Pascale and Athos, 1981) and *In Search of Excellence* (Peters and Waterman, 1982) into best-sellers.

This was a time of intense competition between management consulting firms like McKinsey and Boston Consulting Group. Consultants saw the potential for developing frameworks that could be sold to corporate clients. Just like in the case of Maslow's pyramid, management academics were keen to be seen as having knowledge that was relevant to business. Initially, many academics were critical of pop-management, which they believed was based on anecdotes and catchy slogans rather than rigorous academic research. However, academics soon came to realise that if they ignored popular management ideas they risked being regarded as irrelevant by managers in the 'real world', so they began to include popular management ideas in their textbooks.

There was another factor unique to the change-as-three-steps case. Before change management existed, the field most concerned with change in organizations was called organizational development (OD). By the 1980s, a growing group of academics, consultants, publishers and managers interested in change, criticized OD for being preoccupied with humanistic and democratic values. OD practitioners typically adopted the role of 'facilitator' or 'process consultant' – roles that were not considered senior executive positions. This encouraged the emergence of a rival, more business-oriented, strategic approach referred to as 'change management'.

This new sub-field of change management needed a history to give it credibility. And this history needed a founder. Lewin was the ideal choice: one of the twentieth century's most innovative social scientists, with an outstanding track record of theory development based on solid experimentation and lengthy empirical observation. By the end of the 1980s, Lewin's 'change as three steps' – a seemingly common-sense, but apparently academically proven *and* valuable tool for leaders – would become the foundation of change management. It ticked all the boxes, providing just the kind of theoretical content that management text-books in the 1980s were looking for.

Resistance to change

Let's return to the concept of restraining forces, which was part of Lewin's force-field model. John Kotter, who gave us the popular eight-step model for transforming organizations, has provided the field of change management with another memorable and widely applied framework; this one on resistance to change. In contrast to the universal prescription of the eight steps, Kotter's resistance to change framework, created with Leonard Schlesinger and published in *Harvard Business Review* in 1979, is a contingency theory, where the correct approach for overcoming change depends on the who is resisting, for what reasons, and the power they have for undermining the change.

Kotter and Schlesinger's theory outlines four common reasons why people resist change:

- They might lose something as a result of the change (potentially their job). Their resistance is seen to be a selfish act, because they focus on what is best for them rather than what is best for the organization.
- They don't understand why change is necessary, or they don't trust the leaders.
- They have a different assessment of the merit of the change.
- They have a low tolerance for change and fear not being able to adapt to it.

Kotter and Schlesinger then outline various approaches for dealing with resistance. For example, in situations where resistance is the result of people not understanding the rationale for the change, education and communication is the best approach. In cases where those resisting the change are powerful, change leaders should involve them in design-ing the change and be prepared to negotiate with them to gain their support. However, when the change leaders are powerful and speed is essential, Kotter and Schlesinger's advice to leaders is to force resistors to accept the change by threatening them, transferring them or, if necessary, firing them.

Harvard Business Review reprinted Kotter and Schlesinger's article in 2008 because of its continued influence and it remains one of the frameworks best remembered by management students. It can be criticized, however, for providing a highly one-sided view of resistance. While it states that those affected by the change can be driven by self-interest (resisting the change because they will lose out), it assumes that the leaders of change do not act in self-interest. Leaders are always seen to be doing what they think is best for the organization. We think it would be unwise, and perhaps a little naïve, to make this assumption. Might it not be possible that leaders propose change because they will gain something as a result?

Think again about the popular distinction between 'change leadership' and 'status quo management' that we described at the beginning of the chapter. Our students all wanted to be 'leaders' rather than 'managers' because of the value judgements placed on these roles. Given that this way of thinking about leadership and management is so pervasive today, shouldn't we acknowledge the possibility that senior executives might be incentivized to create transformational change programmes in order to be seen as 'leaders'?

It is worth noting that neither Lewin's nor Kotter's change theories (as they are presented) have a step which involves determining whether change is in fact necessary and/or desirable for the organization (although Lewin himself did endorse such an approach as a result of the Harwood studies). There is no diagnosis stage in those theories, just a prescription. It would be like your doctor prescribing you medicine without first trying to find out what is wrong with you. Maybe there is nothing wrong with you at all. Also, neither Lewin's nor Kotter's change models involve assessing whether the change was successful and produced benefits for the organization. Returning to the doctor analogy, it would be like your doctor continuing to prescribe the same medicine without checking that it is helping alleviate your symptoms.

As we've discussed already, the message in these theories is that change is good, leaders make it happen, and more is better. Once you've finished one change, or even before then, you should start another.

This 'pro-change bias' in our commonly applied management theories might be contributing to two responses to change that are receiving increasing attention by researchers – change fatigue and cynicism. Eric Abrahamson (2004) challenges the popular mantra which says that in an increasingly competitive business environment those organizations which are not continuously changing will perish. He believes that in organizations that undergo too much change, too fast, it can be a case of 'change and perish'. Abrahamson describes 'repetitive change syndrome', characterized by too many change initiatives, change-related chaos, cynicism and burnout.

Cynicism is best understood as a loss of faith in the leaders of change and can be a response to employees' experience of change in the past (Reichers et al., 1997). They might have been in the organization for many years and seen chief executives arrive with transformational change programmes, only to move on after a short time to be replaced by another leader with their own grand vision for the organization. Or, employees might have become cynical about change leaders over-promising and under-delivering.

While we are seeing more research questioning the pro-change bias that is baked into the field's most well-known theories, we are yet to see this diversity of thought reflected in best-selling textbooks, which remain wedded to a unitarist, managerialist perspective. This provides a one-sided, and therefore – we would argue – unrealistic, depiction of organizational life that ill-prepares students for managerial careers.

One of the ways we can think more critically in this respect is to focus on what Learmonth and Morrell (2019) call the 'language of leadership'. For instance:

- What do we mean when we label an action as 'leadership'?
- When we talk about the need for strong leadership, what exactly do we mean by 'strong'? What assumptions are we making or perpetuating?

In the next section, we focus on the language of leadership, especially as it pertains to gender.

Leadership and gender as social constructions

Amanda Sinclair (2005, 2007) starts down this path with the observation that while so much is written about leadership, relatively little attention is given to examining women and leadership. When it is discussed, the emphasis is on explaining why women are underrepresented in leadership roles.

Sinclair calls this the 'absence argument' because it focuses on women in offering explanations for their absence. The absence argument can take various forms – a denial that this is in fact a problem, or that the problem is women (in that they need to learn how to lead like men), or that what is needed is to promote women into senior roles so they can serve as role models for other women.

Sinclair's theorizing encourages us to look beyond the absence argument to consider what we understand 'leadership' to mean. The theory of social constructionism, which we introduced earlier in the book, informs this view. Social constructionism holds that the meanings we attach to particular concepts, such as 'leadership', are produced by interactions between people in a particular social context (time and place). However, there is a tendency for these meanings (or constructs) to be seen as natural, or common sense, rather than the result of social processes that can be reinterpreted and redefined.

Because most of our leaders throughout history have been seen by men to be men, Sinclair argues that our definition of good leadership is a masculine construction. Thus, the dominant view is that leaders are assertive, competitive risk-takers – characteristics that we associate with men. This makes it unlikely that a more feminine style of leading, which emphasizes empathy, nurturing and care, will be regarded as 'leadership' because it does not conform to our definition of what 'leadership' is.

Sinclair labels this social constructionist explanation the 'invisibility argument' – it's not that women's leadership is absent; it's just not recognized. The negative effects on women in the workplace are compounded because the social construction of leadership puts pressure on women to act like men in order to be judged as 'real leaders'. Yet when they do so, those behaviours are evaluated differently. So, for example, when a man is assertive, he's likely to described as a 'leader', but when a woman is assertive, she's likely to be labelled 'bossy'.

From the perspective of the invisibility argument, the issue is not just about getting more women into senior positions. The United Kingdom has had two female Prime Ministers: Margaret Thatcher and Theresa May. It's likely that neither would have got to the top without conforming to the dominant, masculine style of leadership in UK politics. And this is not just an issue about women. The implication of Sinclair's argument is that men who exhibit feminine styles are also less likely to be regarded as leaders.

We should also keep in mind that different cultures support different views of what good leadership is. For example, many indigenous traditions support more communal decision making and leadership, and many from these backgrounds express difficulty in trying to conform to Western and male models.

Like all positions informed by social constructionism theory, there is optimism about the possibilities of change. Constructions are shared understandings that are created by social interactions, which means they can also change over time. Just because 'leadership' has been dominated by masculinity in the past does not mean it need be that way in the future. In New Zealand, Jacinda Ardern was elected Prime Minister in 2017 and has been hailed as offering a new progressive and inclusive style of leadership.

Ardern became only the world's second elected head of government to give birth while in office, with her daughter cared for at home by her partner. And she gained international acclaim for her response to a terrorist attack in Christchurch in 2019, in which a gunman murdered 51 Muslims at two mosques. Ardern was praised for her empathy with the grieving Muslim community and a photo of her dressed in a hijab was shared around the world. Perhaps this is one sign that our understanding of what is 'strong leadership' is beginning to shift.

A more recent theoretical development emphasizes the need to 'queer' leadership. This argues that those who emphasize feminine leadership, such as Sinclair, often rely on stereotypical understandings of masculine and feminine that are tied to sex. Muhr and Sullivan (2013: 419) note that 'gender is understood as a binary where "man" is read against "woman", and sex and gender are conflated to mean the same thing and assumed heterosexual'. A female body is expected to exhibit femininity, and those who transgress these norms are seen as abnormal. By queering leadership, Muhr and Sullivan set out to disrupt this heteronormative view on gender by seeing gender as a social construction. Through their study of a transgender leader, they demonstrate how it is possible for any leader to be judged on their merits rather than according to dominant gendered constructions.

Conclusion

In this chapter, we've examined theories of leadership and change, two of the most popular topics in management today. We've questioned the obsession with personality-based leadership and how this leads to a glorification of transformational change in organizations. This critical exploration of theories of leadership and change can, we believe, open us to new ways of thinking.

Critical insights

13. *Simplistic distinctions between 'leadership' and 'management' are unhelpful.*

Academics and business consultants have profited from promoting the theory that leadership and management are different – that leaders are great people who transform organizations, while managers are deficient in skill and courage and cling to the status quo. However, this simplistic binary does not capture the complexity of managing organizations.

14. *Collective forms of leadership can overcome the dangers of individual-based approaches.*

There were good reasons why personality-based theories of leadership fell out of favour. People who are charismatic and visionary can pull in followers and gain high levels of commitment. While the field of leadership may want to pretend that only those with 'good' and 'moral' visions are leaders, the examples of Hitler, Stalin and Mussolini show that there is a dark side to transformational leadership. We should be wary of placing too much power in the hands of any individual and recognize the potential of more democratic forms of managing organizations.

15. *Challenging the origins of change management theory provides a more balanced view of stability and change.*

The foundations of change management are based on a narrow set of assumptions: that change is good, that more is better, and that those who create change care about the organization while those who resist change care only about themselves. These theories provide a partial and misleading understanding of organizational reality and have gained legitimacy through the embellishment of Lewin's writing. Creating new foundations, which take a more balanced view on the desirability of change and the motivations of both 'leaders' and 'resistors', would enable better theories of change dynamics to be discovered.

16. *Challenging common-sense theories of what good leadership is can inspire new thinking.*

Amanda Sinclair's thinking informs us that one of the consequences of a past where most of our leaders have been men is that we have been conditioned to think of leadership in masculine terms. This social construction serves the interests of men and marginalizes women, who are under pressure to lead like men but are likely to be evaluated negatively when they do. Queering leadership further encourages us to think about gender as a social construction and therefore to resist the conflation of sex and gender. There is an opportunity for leadership to be more strongly associated with femininity, but we should not reduce this to something that is expected of, and necessarily performed by, women.

Search *VSFI Management Theory* in YouTube to watch videos relating to each critical insight.

6

The Rise of Ethics and Corporate Social Responsibility

If you studied management 40 years ago, your textbook probably would not have had a chapter devoted to ethics and corporate social responsibility (CSR). In the 1980s, a commonly-held view was that 'business ethics' was an oxymoron – that people didn't succeed in business by being ethical, because business was about doing what made you money, rather than esoteric questions of right and wrong.

Today, ethics and CSR may be the most talked about topics in business. Whether it is the actions that organizations are taking to reduce their carbon footprint, or to improve the ethical practices in their supply chain, organizations increasingly want to be seen as taking their societal responsibilities seriously.

Business ethics and CSR have gone mainstream and are now core topics in management textbooks. Samson et al. (2018: 186) define business ethics as 'the moral principles and values that govern the behaviour of managers with respect to what is right or wrong'. CSR is defined as the 'obligations of management to enhance the welfare and interests of society, as well as of the organization' (Samson et al., 2018: 198). There is an assumption here, which we return to later in the chapter, of a win–win scenario: that when managers act responsibly, they benefit both business *and* society.

A common starting point for management textbooks is to refer to a series of corporate scandals that occurred at the start of the twenty-first century. The biggest of these scandals was Enron. In 2001, it emerged that the energy company, named by *Fortune* magazine 'America's most innovative company' for six years in a row between 1996 and 2001, was involved in corruption and accounting fraud. The company created artificial power shortages in California in order to charge excessive prices. When its financial performance worsened, assets and profits were inflated, and the company's high level of debt was hidden from investors. Enron eventually went bankrupt, costing stockholders US$74 billion in the process. In the aftermath, chief executive Jeff Skilling, a graduate of Harvard Business School, was sentenced to 24 years in jail and the company's auditor, Arthur Andersen, lost its licence to offer public accounting services.

The crisis which swept financial markets in 2008, leading to the collapse of major financial services firms, such as Bear Stearns and Lehman Brothers, prompted another round of questioning over the morality of executives. While the causes of the crisis were varied and complex, particular attention focused on the risks that senior executives had taken to maximize profits in the short term. When the global financial system went into meltdown, governments stepped in with rescue packages and bailouts paid for with taxpayer money.

The global financial crisis intensified concerns that had been growing since the Enron scandal about the moral shortcomings of business school graduates. Business schools were blamed for producing 'wannabe Gordon Geckos', the character played by Michael Douglas in Oliver Stone's 1987 film *Wall Street*, whose catchphrase 'greed is good' typified the recklessness and lack of morals exhibited by Wall Street in the 1980s. Khurana (2007) lamented that business schools had abandoned the idea of management as a profession with 'higher aims', in favour of a view which sees managers as 'hired hands' serving stockholder interests.

The response from the business education sector was swift. The Association to Advance Collegiate Schools of Business (AACSB), which provides quality assurance and accreditation to business schools, announced that teaching business ethics should be a top priority. Harvard Business School led the way by creating a Hippocratic Oath for Managers, based on that undertaken by medical professionals, in which managers pledge to serve the public interest. Business schools around the world joined the quest, revamping their curriculum and promising to do a better job of producing future managers with a stronger moral compass.

Unfortunately, despite the increased emphasis on business ethics, scandals continue to make headlines. One of the most staggering was the deception staged by Elizabeth Holmes, chief executive of health technology company Theranos. Holmes claimed to have developed a revolutionary blood testing technology using tiny volumes of blood, an innovation inspired by her own fear of needles. By 2015, Holmes topped Forbes' list of richest self-made women, her wealth estimated at US$4.5 billion.

However, it subsequently emerged that the technology could not do what was claimed and that Holmes was involved in the cover-up. She and the company were charged with massive fraud and the company was forced to close. Holmes' story, told in a documentary film *The Investor: Out for Blood in Silicon Valley* (2019, HBO) illustrates the dark, immoral side of transformational leadership. Holmes had created a cult of personality at Theranos. It was a company where employees who believed in the fantasy were rewarded and those who raised concerns were ostracized.

Another recent jaw-dropper was the Volkswagen (VW) emissions scandal. In 2015, the US Environmental Protection Agency found that many VW cars sold in America had a 'defeat device' installed to detect when the car was being tested for emissions of harmful gases. The software enabled the car to emit up to 40 times lower levels of gases during the test compared with when they were driven on the road. VW owners, many of whom were environmentally conscious and had purchased the vehicles because of their supposed low emissions, were outraged.

After repeatedly denying the existence of defeat devices, VW came clean. The company was fined US$2.8 billion, 10 million vehicles were recalled and chief executive Martin Winterkorn resigned. Perhaps the most disturbing aspect of the scandal was captured in the Netflix documentary series *Dirty Money: Hard Nox* (2018). It alleged that the German government knew that defeat devices were being used and turned a blind eye because of the importance of the automobile industry to the country's economy.

Carroll's pyramid of CSR

Probably the most-well known theory in the topic of ethics is Archie Carroll's pyramid of CSR, shown in Figure 6.1 (Carroll, 1991). As with Maslow's pyramid of human needs, we think the pyramid symbol has contributed significantly to the enduring popularity of Carroll's framework. Unlike Maslow, Carroll did actually build the pyramid that bears his name!

The pyramid is made up four levels of responsibilities.

At the base are *economic* responsibilities, commonly understood as the responsibility to maximize profit. To be sustainable, a business must be profitable. Only then can it continue to provide jobs for employees, to provide the goods and services that customers need and to deliver on the responsibilities at higher levels of the pyramid.

A business must be profitable, but it must obey the law in generating those profits. These *legal* responsibilities make up the second level of the pyramid. Carroll sees legal responsibilities as reflecting 'codified ethics' – that is, the law reflects societal expectations of what is fair and just business conduct. Laws are like the rules of a game – winning is the objective, but to win you must play by the rules. We will return to this analogy later when we discuss the role that government plays in setting these rules and the actions businesses take in attempting to influence the rule-making process.

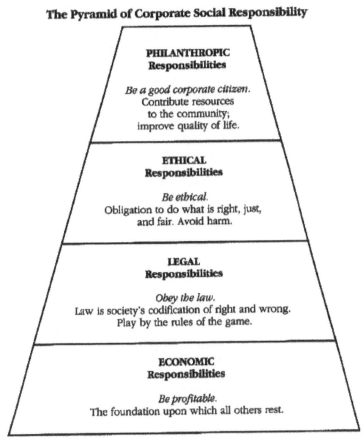

Figure 6.1   Carroll's pyramid of corporate social responsibility

(Source: Carroll, 1991: 42)

The next level up consists of those responsibilities that are expected by society but are not codified into law. These *ethical* responsibilities might comprise changing ethics or values championed by social movements. For example, it has become common for organizations to make commitments to becoming carbon neutral even though this is not required by law. This might be because they genuinely believe it is the right thing to do in response to climate change, or because they are under pressure from environmentally conscious customers.

At the top of the pyramid are *philanthropic* responsibilities, which reflect society's expectation for organizations to be 'good corporate citizens' and might include donations of money or time to charities or community activities. Philanthropic responsibilities are desirable, but Carroll's theory suggests that firms are not unethical if they do not perform them.

Carroll's pyramid is a useful theory for thinking about business ethics. We see that Theranos and VW neglected their ethical and legal responsibilities in the pursuit of higher profits. The pyramid is also appealing for textbook authors because it purports to offer something new. Carroll (1991: 40) says, 'to be sure, all these responsibilities have always existed to some extent, but it has only been in recent years that ethical and philanthropic functions have taken a significant place'.

This creates the impression that while some businesses, like Theranos and VW, are unethical, these are unusual cases, or 'bad apples', among a majority of companies following good practice. Students are reassured that the business community is for the first time in history taking social responsibilities seriously. Students are further reassured that the increased emphasis on CSR proves that businesses are more ethical than ever. So, all's well, no need to be alarmed.

In this chapter, we challenge this narrative. We explore some popular ethical theories and show that while they promote an ideal of the ethical manager, they have blind-spots that ignore important aspects of ethics, such as power relationships in organizations and the role of government in regulating organizational behaviour. By taking a historical perspective, we show that debates about the morality of business executives and the responsibilities of business are as old as business itself. We highlight some periods where these debates assumed great importance and argue that a better understanding of this past provides us an opportunity to think differently today. First, however, we turn our attention to Milton Friedman, another famous theorist on CSR.

Friedman versus Freeman

Milton Friedman was an intellectual leader of the so-called Chicago school of economics, a school of thought that challenged Keynesian economics, an economic theory that saw government needing to play an active role in the economy. Friedman was a staunch advocate of a free market economic system with minimal government intervention, and he was an advisor to both US President Ronald Reagan and UK Prime Minister Margaret Thatcher during the 1980s. Friedman's 1962 book,

Capitalism and Freedom, was a best-seller, but in terms of CSR, he is best remembered for his 1970 article in *The New York Times* and his famous statement that 'the social responsibility of business is to increase its profits'.

Friedman argued that corporate executives are employed by the business owners and therefore have a responsibility 'to make as much money as possible while conforming to the basic rules of society, both those embodied in law and those embodied in ethical custom' (Friedman, 1970). Friedman is vague on what he means by 'ethical custom', but he certainly does not want businesses to engage in philanthropy, such as making donations of money to charity. Profits should be maximized and returned to owners, he theorized. Those owners can then choose to support worthy causes if they wish.

In management textbooks, Friedman's view is often characterized as the 'stockholder view' and is contrasted with Edward Freeman's 'stakeholder view'. Freeman's 1984 book, *Strategic Management: A Stakeholder Approach*, argues that successful businesses develop their strategy around relationships with those who have a stake (or interest) in the organization.

- Employees have a stake because they spend much of their lives at work and derive an income from it.
- Customers have a stake because they rely on the goods or services provided.
- Local communities, government and the environment, and of course the owners, all have a stake.

In the narrative preferred by today's management textbooks, Freeman is the hero and Friedman the villain. We are told that Friedman failed to recognize that society expects more of business than maximizing profits within the law. In contrast, Freeman recognizes that executives should balance the interests of all stakeholders rather than single-handedly pursue the narrow financial interest of stockholders. Carroll's pyramid provides a practical tool for managing these responsibilities. Carroll's claim that ethical and philanthropic responsibilities are novel provides the historical narrative of progress that, as we have seen throughout this book, appeals to textbook authors. The story is one of the field of management maturing and promoting a more enlightened approach to managing over time.

This is a reassuring story for those who aspire to a managerial career, but the 'new versus old', 'good versus evil' framing of the Freeman versus Friedman debate is rather misleading. Textbooks position Friedman as the 'bad guy', yet the free market ideology he promoted continues to be supported by business schools. Why, then, does Friedman get labelled the 'bad guy' in management textbooks? Because he provides a theory that justifies the development of CSR as the most advanced theory of business ethics.

According to Edward Wray-Bliss (2017), it is no coincidence that ethics and CSR became popular under a version of capitalism that regards government intervention in the economy as inefficient and largely unnecessary. In free market thinking, governments should hand over responsibilities to business leaders, who are encouraged to 'self-' or 'voluntarily' regulate. To return to the 'rules of the game' analogy outlined earlier, it's like the referee allowing the players to make up their own rules and encouraging them to follow those rules but without forcing them to do so.

Deregulation is welcomed by the business community because it leads to a reduction of governmental bureaucratic 'red tape'. In return, business leaders reassure society that the trust placed in them by society is warranted. This seems like a win–win situation – business operates largely free from government intervention, the costs to taxpayers falls because less people are needed to create and enforce regulations, and society benefits from organizations being socially responsible as depicted in Carroll's pyramid.

There's good reason to question, therefore, textbooks' portrayal of Friedman's theory as outdated and irrelevant. We think it remains highly relevant for the field of management, because it provides the intellectual justification for the growth of business ethics and CSR – it is an important link in the same chain.

We can also question the portrayal in management textbooks of Friedman and Freeman having theories that oppose each other – the stockholder approach *versus* the stakeholder approach. We think they are more similar than different. Best-selling textbooks create the impression that Freeman developed stakeholder theory to compete with Friedman's stockholder theory. But as Walsh (2005) points out, Freeman's book *Strategic Management* is about business strategy, not corporate social responsibility – it was only later repurposed as a theory of ethics.

Freeman argued that the growing complexity and globalization of the business environment in the 1980s meant that executives needed to monitor closely their external environment to account for all those affected by the organization's actions. In other words, Freeman was primarily concerned with how to make money, not how to be a good corporate citizen. Freeman openly acknowledges in a subsequent book (Freeman et al., 2010: 12): 'Both we and Friedman agree that business and capitalism are not about social responsibility. We contend that stakeholder theory is about business and value creation, and, as we have said, it is managerial.'

Freeman, like Friedman, adopts a managerial perspective in seeing that the primary aim of organizations is to maximize profits. For Freeman, that is best done by having 'great products and services that customers want, solid relationships with suppliers that keep operations on the cutting edge, inspired employees who stand for the company mission and push the company to become better, and supportive communities that allow businesses to flourish' (Freeman et al., 2010: 11). Both Freeman and Friedman are unitarists who believe that executives have the right to decide how best to manage the business. Both believe in small government – that government should hand over responsibilities to business, and that business can be trusted to act responsibly.

Do Freeman and Friedman actually disagree on anything? Freeman believes that if Friedman were alive today, he'd be a stakeholder theorist, as it is now largely accepted that corporations which contribute to worthy projects in the community themselves benefit – through positive publicity and the generation of goodwill among their stakeholders. It is also recognized that when corporations are seen to have acted unethically, it can hurt them financially. A close reading of Friedman reveals he did understand this 'enlightened self-interest' – that by furthering the interests of others, businesses ultimately serve their own interest. But he thought it dishonest for businesses to disguise their self-interest under the 'cloak of social responsibility'. He also saw it as short-sighted, because while business gained kudos in the short term 'it helps strengthen the already too prevalent view that the pursuit of profits is wicked and immoral' (Friedman, 1970).

The manager as ethical decision maker

We've seen already why business ethics and CSR have been embraced by the business community. Profitable business and ethics are seen to be compatible, rather than a contradiction in terms. By business recognizing their social responsibilities, it becomes less likely that governments will create laws and regulations that burden free enterprise. As Wray-Bliss (2017) puts it, for managers the problem of relevance (why should we take ethics seriously?) has been answered (because it is in our financial interests to do so).

A second problem facing theories of business ethics is the problem of conscience. Who should decide what ethics are relevant? Individuals are encouraged to behave ethically by their conscience, or out of fear of

God, but who should be the conscience of the organization? You can probably guess the answer to that – management. This helps explain the popularity of theories such as transformational and authentic leadership that we discussed in Chapter 5. These theories assume that senior executives are of high moral standing – they do what is right, just and good, and it is therefore they who should define and enforce the organization's ethics. Unfortunately, when they turn out to be cheats, like Enron's Jeff Skilling or Theranos' Elizabeth Holmes, the damage to organizations, countries, citizens and stakeholders can be enormous.

If management are the ethical conscience of the organization, then they need frameworks to make decisions about how to resolve ethical dilemmas. Management textbooks provide a range of theories from the field of moral philosophy that can be used to inform ethical decision making. Textbooks vary in their coverage, but the four theoretical perspectives most often used are utilitarianism, deontology, justice ethics and virtue ethics.

In utilitarianism, which originates from Jeremy Bentham and John Stuart Mill, the ethical value of an act is based on its consequences. An ethical act is that which leads to the greatest good for the greatest number. This is a common approach to moral reasoning in business because it seeks to account for costs and benefits, but it has trouble accounting for individual rights.

Deontology, associated with German philosopher Immanuel Kant, uses rules to determine right from wrong, which makes it different to utilitarianism's focus on consequences. Kant believed ethical actions followed universal moral rules such as 'do not commit murder'. Following rules makes deontology easy to apply but its weakness is ignoring consequences. Sometimes, might not be breaking a rule be the right thing to do, to prevent a terrible outcome?

Justice-based approaches to ethics, formulated by John Locke, are similar to deontology in seeking to establish universal rights, but they differ by focusing on the issue of fairness, which is tricky because it can mean different things to different people.

Virtue ethics, which is traced back to Aristotle and other Ancient Greeks, focuses on the character of the person who acts. It focuses on what it means to be a virtuous human being and considers the moral character of managers.

As Martin Parker (2002) observes, this impressive line-up of famous moral philosophers provides the sub-field of business ethics with gravitas. In addition, moral philosophers are appealing for management textbooks because their theories can be reduced to a tool that managers can use to resolve ethical dilemmas. Parker encourages us to consider the philosophers that do not get mentioned in best-selling management textbooks. References to twentieth-century continental philosophers such as Foucault and Friedrich Nietzsche are rare, as is the inclusion of Marxist perspectives that we introduced earlier.

Including these theorists would enable students to explore issues of power, justice and equality and to examine how an economic system which incentivizes profit maximization can encourage unethical actions. It would enable a closer examination of government's responsibility for regulating business conduct. That is important because government sets 'the rules of the game' that organizations play by and determines the extent to which those rules are enforced. As we saw earlier, it was suggested that VW's cheating was emboldened by managers' belief that the German government would turn a blind eye because of the company's contribution to the economy.

Does the growth of CSR mean that organizational behaviour is more ethical?

Given the increasing attention that business ethics and CSR is receiving, it might be assumed that organizational behaviour is becoming more ethical. It is certainly a plausible argument to make. Businesses have an incentive to act with responsibility because they realize that if they don't, government will step in to strengthen legal requirements.

This threat of regulation is regularly used by government in circumstances where it feels business is not self-regulating adequately. In New Zealand, the government has threatened to introduce a sugar tax on fizzy drinks to address an escalating obesity and type 2 diabetes epidemic. But before actually acting on this, it hopes that the food and drink industry will respond by taking voluntary steps to reduce sugar content. This has begun to happen, with drink manufacturers discovering that there is demand for reduced-sugar products.

However, there is also a plausible argument that more CSR does not make business more ethical. Wray-Bliss describes this as the 'corporate takeover of ethics', where 'ethics is reduced to a corporate image exercise in support of the business drive for profits' (2017: 581).

An example of this is 'greenwashing', where organizations (such as VW) promote themselves and their products as environmentally friendly, while their actual environmental practices suggest otherwise. Businesses who greenwash want the benefits that come with being seen to be green without the cost or effort of acting green, and it is a practice that is becoming more common as consumer demand for environmentally sound goods and services grows.

Not only might we consider greenwashing to be unethical (and in the case of VW, illegal), it reduces the likelihood of more radical change. If these businesses were more honest about their intentions not to take genuine action to reduce the negative effect on the environment, then governments might be more likely to enforce change through regulatory and other legal avenues. CSR, then, can act as a valve that releases pressure for more substantial change.

A second argument that explains why more CSR does not necessarily mean more ethical organizations comes from sociologist Zygmunt Bauman, who believed that giving managers the power to define and enforce the ethics of the organization might actually increase unethical organizational practices. For Bauman (1989), ethics should be the responsibility of individuals, not decided on their behalf by management. He believed 'the organization as a whole is an instrument to obliterate responsibility' (Bauman, 1989: 163), because employees are under pressure to obey orders issued by those above them in the hierarchy. This supresses individual responsibility.

The dangers of obedience to authority were highlighted by Stanley Milgram (1974) in a series of experiments conducted at Yale University during the 1960s. Participants in Milgram's experiments thought they were taking part in a study on the effects of punishment on learning. They were given the role of 'teacher' and ordered by an authority figure (somebody dressed in a white lab coat) to administer electric shocks to a 'learner' strapped to a chair, beginning at 15 volts and increasing after each incorrect answer to 450 volts. The studies were designed to see how far participants would go before refusing to obey. The results surprised and dismayed Milgram, with 65 per cent of participants going all the way to 450 volts.

How can such extreme levels of cruelty by otherwise decent people be explained? In the debrief following the experiment, many participants refused to accept responsibility for their actions, saying they were just doing what they were told. It was the man in the white coat, they said, who was responsible.

But there is more to it than just authority relations, as Milgram discovered by modifying the experiment so that the 'teachers' were further removed from the consequence of their decisions. When participants had only to administer the test, while another person delivered the shock, 92.5 per cent of them continued to the maximum voltage. From this we can see the dangers of the division of labour, one of the enduring theories of management we examined in Chapter 2.

Hierarchy of authority and the division of labour are pervasive features of today's organizations. If you're far removed from the consequences of your decisions, or if you're just following orders from your boss without question, there is the potential for unethical behaviour. Just because organizations have become more active in CSR does not ensure that organizational behaviour is more ethical.

Constructing earlier foundations of business ethics and CSR

Students of best-selling introductory textbooks in management could be forgiven for thinking that before Friedman and Freeman, nobody in business had given much thought to issues of social responsibility. As we saw earlier, Carroll, the creator of the CSR pyramid in 1991, believed ethical and philanthropic responsibilities were being taken seriously by organizations for the first time in history. Samson et al.'s (2018: 206) textbook says Friedman's profit-maximizing view is 'no longer considered an adequate criterion of social performance', implying corporations' recognition of social responsibilities is something new.

However, if we look back further into the past, we see that debates about the morality of business executives and the responsibilities of business are centuries old. In the remainder of this chapter we highlight three cases where these debates assumed great importance. We first examine the Quakers and their distinctive paternalistic approach to business. We then discuss the great US industrialists of the nineteenth century, who some people call great philanthropists, and others 'robber barons'. Finally, we consider what business schools might learn from the past about their role in holding business to account for its impact on society.

The Quakers: Forgotten pioneers of ethical business?

The Quaker movement gave us some of today's iconic family businesses: Cadbury's chocolate (1824), accounting firm Price Waterhouse (1865) (now Price Waterhouse Coopers, or PWC), and biscuit companies Huntley and Palmer (1822) and Jacobs (1851). Kavanagh and Brigham (2018) point out that while the Quakers' success is widely recognized in the field of general history, it is largely missing from the history of management. Remember from Chapter 2 that many textbooks suggest management theory to be little more than a century old. The Quaker movement dates back much further and was pivotal, argue Kavanagh and Brigham, in advancing theories of ethical business.

Quakerism emerged as a religious movement in England in the seventeenth century. Quakers, also called Friends, believe in the idea of 'God in everyone', often referred to as the 'Inner Light'. They believe that everyone can have a direct relationship with, and experience of, God without the need for religious rituals or hierarchy. The Quakers had remarkable business success in Britain and also in the US – Frederick Taylor was a Quaker, as was Mary Parker Follett and Joseph Wharton, who founded America's first business school, the Wharton School in Pennsylvania in 1881.

Wharton was a major stockholder in Bethlehem Steel Corporation, the company made famous for employing Frederick Taylor in 1898 to run his experiment with 'Schmidt' to illustrate his scientific approach to management. The Quakers were innovators and modernizers and much of their business success was based on developing new technologies and processes, which could be scientifically proven to be effective.

The most famous Quaker firm was Cadbury, the British confectionary company owned by Mondelez International (previously Kraft Foods). Until 1962, it was a private company owned and managed by members of the Cadbury family. The business was started by John Cadbury in 1824 in the centre of Birmingham. Initially, the focus was the tea and coffee trade, but after struggling in these markets the Cadbury family began concentrating on cocoa and chocolate production. In 1879, as a response to poor working and living conditions in Birmingham's city centre and a desire to expand the business, Cadbury built a new factory at Bournville, a greenfield site on the outskirts of the city. Houses were built for the workers and sold at cost price, with mortgages available from Cadbury. Surrounding the factory were community facilities, including schools, parks, recreation grounds and other amenities.

The Quaker ethic was the cornerstone of Cadbury's (Dellheim, 1987). Guided by their religious beliefs, they were enlightened employees for their time, seeing workers as humans rather than cogs in a machine. They also believed workers should have a say in the running of the business, developing a scheme where employees could make suggestions for improving products and processes as well as their working conditions. They provided education classes for workers and encouraged them to get involved with the social life of Bournville. The Cadbury family took a paternalistic role, believing that they knew what was best for their staff. They had a unitarist frame of reference – they did not welcome trade unions or government interfering in their relationship with their employees.

Changes in UK corporate law in the mid-nineteenth century introduced the limited liability form of ownership, which meant that the private assets of business owners were not at risk if the company failed.

The Quakers welcomed this change as an opportunity to expand their family businesses, but growth meant that new managers needed to be hired, many of whom either did not know or care much about Quaker aspirations. The result was a loss of family control and an eventual dilution of Quaker business practices.

So what can we learn from the Quakers? They showed that an explicitly moral approach to running a business, together with a long-term view, was a successful strategy. Another useful lesson is that scientific management and a concern for people could co-exist. The Quakers were deeply concerned with the intrinsic needs of their employees, but they also welcomed the efficiency gains made by scientific management. This was their approach decades before the experiments at Hawthorne, providing further proof that Mayo's 'discovery' that workers have social needs was not really a discovery after all.

Finally, the case of the Quakers shows the circularity of management theories. In the 1960s, Cadbury was advised by the management consulting firm McKinsey to move away from catering for every need of their workers, since this came at a substantial cost and McKinsey did not believe it generated sufficient revenues. Today, however, the idea of 'company towns' in the Bournville tradition is making a comeback. With the rapid upswing in house prices across the world, companies like New Zealand bed manufacturer Sleepyhead are relocating their factories to the countryside, where they can provide affordable housing and other amenities to their employees.

A paternalistic approach to running business has also made a comeback in the form of the 'business campus' popularized by Google and Apple. Google regularly tops 'best places to work' surveys by providing everything that its workers might need during the day. In addition to a gymnasium and recreation spaces, there is free high-quality food, hairdressers, masseuses and washing machines. Employees can even take their dog to work. Of course, there is a quid pro quo – without a need to leave work, employees can work longer hours. The absence of a religious conviction may distinguish Google from the Quakers, but as some business commentators have observed, the strong identification with the firm that Google elicits from its employees makes working there something akin to a religious experience.

Robber barons or great philanthropists? Or both?

In 2015, Facebook's founder Mark Zuckerberg and his wife Priscilla Chan pledged to donate 99 per cent of their Facebook stock, then valued at US\$45 billion, over the course of their lives to the Chan Zuckerberg Initiative, a limited liability company that would focus on improving health and education.

Zuckerberg received high praise for this extraordinarily generous gift and commitment to help those in need. Others, however, were sceptical about his motives. Facebook has been caught up in numerous controversies over the privacy of data it collects on users. The highest-profile case, in 2018, involved Cambridge Analytica, a political consulting firm which collected data and used it to advise candidates running for office, including Donald Trump. Cambridge Analytica got hold of the personal data of 87 million Facebook users via a quiz app developed by Aleksandr Kogan, a data scientist who worked as a research associate at the University of Cambridge. Kogan's app, *This is Your Digital Life*, collected data not just from those who agreed to take the quiz, but from all the people in their Facebook network. Facebook was criticized for acting too slowly when they became aware of the breach and for not taking data privacy more seriously.

It has been suggested that Zuckerberg's philanthropy has the effect of shielding himself from criticism over how he has accumulated his enormous wealth. It is also argued that wealthy philanthropists like Zuckerberg are a threat to democracy. Philanthropy, says political theorist Rob Reich (2018), is an act of power, a direct attempt to influence society. The philanthropists' 'play book' is to create a fortune, minimize the taxes they pay to government, complain about the failures of government, declare that they could do a better job, get a tax break by creating a foundation and then expect people to thank them for their genius and generosity. The overall effect, argues Reich, is to weaken the institutions of government, which weakens democracy because while governments are accountable at the ballot box, philanthropists like Zuckerberg are not.

Controversy around corporate philanthropy is nothing new. John D. Rockefeller, who died in 1937 aged 97, is widely considered to be the wealthiest American ever, with his net worth equating to more than 2 per cent of US gross domestic product (GDP) at the time. To put that into context, 2 per cent of US GDP today would equate to \$400 billion. At the time of writing this book, Zuckerberg's wealth was estimated at \$93 billion. In relative terms, Rockefeller was much richer than Microsoft's Bill Gates, Amazon's Jeff Bezos and Zuckerberg combined.

In 1913, when John D. Rockefeller announced he was setting up a philanthropic foundation, former US President Theodore Roosevelt declared 'no amount of charities in spending such fortunes can compensate in any way for the misconduct in acquiring them' (Matthews, 2018).

What had Rockefeller done to invite such scorn? Rockefeller was regarded as one of the 'robber barons' of the second half of the

nineteenth century, a term given to a small group of successful industrialists who were considered to have amassed their fortunes through
unethical activities. Rockefeller founded the Standard Oil Company in
1870 and monopolized the country's oil production, at its peak controlling 90 per cent of supplies. This was at a time when the rapidly expand-
ing US economy was heavily dependent on oil. Electricity had not yet
been introduced and there was a high demand for kerosene used in
lighting. Rockefeller did deals with those who had control over the vital
railroad network to impose charges on competitors who transported oil
by rail. Through his control of the oil that drove the American economy,
Rockefeller expanded his empire.

During this time in American politics, the business practices of the
'robber barons' were attacked by 'muckrakers', investigative journal-
ists who wrote articles for popular American magazines exposing what
they believed was corruption. Ida Tarbell was a leading muckraker
and her history of Standard Oil in 1904 prompted a public backlash
against the company. The US Government responded to the public anger at Rockefeller and other industrialists by creating antitrust
law that broke up their monopolies. Standard Oil was broken up into
more than 30 companies that brought greater competition into the
market.

Rockefeller's public standing fell further with the Ludlow massacre in 1914. In this incident, a number of striking workers, their
wives and children at the Colorado Fuel and Iron Company, which
he controlled, were shot and killed after a seven-month-long strike. It
was considered a key moment in the country's labour relations, with
public anger leading eventually to improved working conditions. The
massacre was said to be an event that awakened Rockefeller's commitment to humanitarian causes. Rockefeller began to take an interest
in employee matters, including helping to fund Mayo's research at
Harvard Business School.

By the time of his death, Rockefeller had given away $500 million,
mostly to medical research and education, but his generosity wasn't
universally welcomed. He was heavily criticized for trying to white-
wash the terrible things he had done to generate his wealth. A 1915
Congressional committee on industrial relations labelled Rockefeller
and Carnegie 'menaces to society'. One member of Congress described
Rockefeller's foundation as 'repugnant to the whole idea of a democratic society' (Matthews, 2018).

In studying business ethics, there is value in looking back to the past
to consider the ethics of philanthropy, as well as responsibilities of government in creating the 'rules of the game' that business operates within.

Was Rockefeller a great philanthropist or a robber baron? Or both? This debate continues today.

Learning from capitalism in crisis: Harvard Dean Donham and the Great Depression

We began this chapter by highlighting the recent interest in business ethics following corporate scandals and the global financial crisis. Business schools have been criticized for being cheerleaders for business and are under pressure to demonstrate that they serve society's interests, rather than the narrower interests of corporations. It would be a mistake to believe that this is a new challenge facing business schools. In this final case, we explore a controversy that played out at Harvard Business School, regarded by many as the ultimate cheerleader for business, a century ago.

We've written already about the Progressive Era, the 20 years leading up until the end of World War I in 1918, where public resentment at laissez-faire capitalism controlled by the 'robber barons' saw government regulate the economy to assist the less well-off in society. Following the war, the situation changed. The sharp deflationary recession of 1919–20 provoked widespread industrial unrest. Workers, represented by unions, demanded better pay and working conditions. Also at this time, there were fears, following the Russian Revolution in 1917, that strikes would lead to a communist revolution in the United States.

It was a volatile combination of factors that resulted in violent clashes between big business and organized labour, with government siding with big business. Marens (2012: 66) concludes that 'the experience of American labour in organizing and confronting the new industrial giants was little short of disastrous'. Unemployment rose, union membership fell rapidly and corporate management found themselves with an extraordinary level of autonomy compared to what was happening in other countries at the time. Victory, however, came at a price, says Marens. With this increased power came societal expectations that business would exercise this power responsibly. The debates taking place at Harvard Business School during this period provide a fascinating insight into how this all played out.

Wallace Donham became Dean of Harvard Business School in 1919, a year when 4 million American workers went on strike (O'Connor, 1999). Donham was a graduate of Harvard's law school and had gone on to work on the receivership of a railway company. This brought him into contact with union members. Inspired by these experiences,

Donham wanted to have the labour view represented in teaching, so he hired Robert Fechner, an influential union leader.

Fechner's appointment angered many. A local industrialist, F.C. Hood, who was a regular guest speaker at the business school, felt it was unwise to have Fechner lecturing impressionable young men, claiming it could sow the seeds of social unrest. In a letter to Donham, Hood (1924) wrote:

> The thought of any department of Harvard having professors who are socialists or Bolshevists or labor unionists is abhorrent to me, especially in these days when some of the very foundations of our Government are being attacked.

Donham was staunch is his defence of Fechner's appointment, since labour issues had been ignored previously and providing this perspective encouraged students to think critically. The Fechner appointment was useful for Donham because the legitimacy of the business school was being questioned by critics who saw the school as a servant of the business community rather than a proper academic department, and which had no place in the university (Veblen, 1918).

Also advantageous was Donham's growing relationship with philosopher Alfred North Whitehead, who had recently joined Harvard's philosophy department. Whitehead (1925) was dismayed by the rapid spread of mass production. Whitehead called on business schools to develop 'foresight' among their students, to enable them to understand and predict social change.

Donham agreed with Whitehead's identification of constant change as the major threat facing Western civilization, and he saw the United States' descent into economic crisis as evidence that this threat was becoming reality. Donham called on business to maintain employment in the face of falling demand and advocated cutting working hours while leaving wages at existing levels, in the hope that undiminished purchasing power combined with additional leisure time would stimulate demand. In this time of crisis, Donham implored business executives to recognize and face their social responsibilities.

> Capitalism is on trial, and, on the issue of this trial may depend the whole future of western civilization. ... Our present situation both here and in all the great industrial nations of the world is a major breakdown of capitalism. Can this be overcome? I believe so, but not without leadership which thinks in terms of broad social problems instead of in terms of particular companies. (Donham, 1932: 207)

The Harvard Crimson commented: 'These ideas are not new, but they have hitherto been considered radical, indeed socialistic, and it is a surprising indication of the progress of the times to hear them from the Dean of a Harvard graduate school' (September 21, 1932).

Donham reshaped the school's curriculum to give greater emphasis to the study of government and its relationship to business, and to business ethics. By the end of 1930s, Harvard was leading the way in a transformation of US business schools which, Khurana (2007: 191) notes, aimed 'to turn business schools into objective analysts and, when necessary, critics of business rather than the apologists and boosters they had been accused of being'. Unfortunately, the transformation lost impetus when a new threat loomed on the horizon – the growing aggression of Germany under Adolf Hitler.

Little is written in management textbooks about this tumultuous period. This is a shame, since it provided fertile ground for the germination of new ways of thinking about business ethics, the relationship between business and society and the role of business schools. There are also strong parallels between that period and the crises of today, including an environmental crisis of climate change and an economic crisis triggered by the Covid-19 pandemic.

Conclusion

Despite many people thinking that topics like sustainability, ethics and CSR are new, and that our theories about them are more advanced than they have ever been, looking back to the past leads us to other conclusions. This can help us to develop new ways of thinking about these important issues.

Critical insights

17. *Milton Friedman and Edward Freeman's theories of Corporate Social Responsibility are not the opposites we are led to believe.*

The standard account of the history of business ethics and CSR starts with Friedman's argument that the only responsibility of business is to maximize its profits. This is regarded as outdated, because Freeman's stakeholder theory teaches us that businesses and managers have responsibilities to others who are impacted by their actions. Rather than seeing Friedman and Freeman as opposing theories, we have argued they have much in common – both are supportive of a managerial perspective and share the corporate goal of profit maximization.

18. *Ethical theories taken from moral philosophy provide insights, but have blind spots.*

Management textbooks provide a range of theories from moral philosophy that can be used to inform ethical decision making. These theories fit well with the managerial perspective that dominates most textbooks. We believe they could be usefully supplemented by philosophical perspectives that pay greater attention to power, inequality and the role of government.

19. *The 'robber barons' and their philanthropy illuminates the social responsibilities of governments and corporations.*

In the late nineteenth century, powerful US corporations were criticized for being too big and powerful and for engaging in unethical practices. This prompted the US government to break up these monopolies through antitrust legislation. Faced with a public backlash, the 'robber barons' leading these corporations became 'great philanthropists' who donated much of their wealth to worthwhile social projects. This debate continues today.

20. *The Quakers adopted a paternalistic approach well before theories about corporate culture emerged.*

The Quakers combined a passion for creating successful businesses with religious beliefs that prioritized nurturing their workers. While their contribution is largely ignored in management history, it can be seen as the foundation of contemporary ideas such as company towns and campus-like workplaces where a wide range of employee benefits and amenities are provided.

Search *VSFI Management Theory* in YouTube to watch videos relating to each critical insight.

7

Conclusion: The Past, Present and Future of Management Theory

> The object was to learn to what extent the effort to think one's own history can free thought from what it silently thinks, and so enable it to think differently.
>
> Michel Foucault (1985: 9)

The past: Questioning the conventional representation of management theory

For more than a decade we have been analyzing how the most familiar names in management theory, including Weber, Smith, Taylor, Maslow and Lewin, are represented in management textbooks. We've compared what best-selling textbooks have to say about these theorists with what they actually wrote. Through this research, we have come to the conclusion that the way in which management's foundational theories are typically presented limits our understanding of what management is and could be.

For instance, it limits management's possibilities by focusing on the *what* of Taylor and scientific management theory and forgetting about the contextual *why* – the desire to use scarce resources wisely. It limits its possibilities by focusing on and celebrating small parts of Adam Smith's writing and leaving out his broader system of thought – an ethical system based on sympathizing with others. It limits us by seeing bureaucracy as either the norm or abhorrent, rather than as a particular form of organizing among a portfolio of other forms. It limits the impact of smart thinkers from the past like Mary Parker Follett by reducing her contribution to bullet points and trite phrases like 'win–win'.

We've published our alternative histories of these theories in academic journals (these are listed in the Appendix). However, as we said in Chapter 1, few people apart from academics read those journals. Moreover, publishing academic papers is not our ultimate goal. We want to influence the way that management is taught at university and, subsequently, how students think about what management can be. If we are able to achieve that, then there is a chance of influencing the way management is practised. This book is as an important step in that journey.

When doing our research on management textbooks, a question that kept coming up was 'why is there such a difference between the original theories and how they are written about in management textbooks?'

We've thought a lot about this question. There are probably many contributing facors and we don't pretend to have identified all of them. One factor is the need for textbooks to condense and simplify theories for students. We've had to do that too in writing this book and can sympathize with textbook authors in this regard.

We also think the misrepresentations are related to how management, as a field of study, has developed over time. It is a young field and so has looked to other disciplines for its theoretical foundations. It found theories in psychology, economics, anthropology, politics, philosophy and sociology, among others. Smith, Weber, Maslow and Lewin were great theorists, but they weren't 'management theorists', so their ideas needed to be repurposed for our field.

The translation of these theories into management is where things have gone awry. These translations have largely been informed by a limited view of what management education should be about, and on a narrow set of ideological beliefs. Let's deal with the limited view first.

The assumed purpose of management education that underpins most textbooks is to train students to be future managers. They are written from the perspective of the manager and theories are presented as 'tools' that managers can utilize to solve problems and improve organizational performance. There is nothing wrong with that *per se*, but it does result in misrepresentations. Maslow's hierarchy of needs is taught to management students as a tool for increasing employee motivation in business, but that is not what Maslow intended it to be.

We think this conventional 'managerial perspective' is best supplemented with an 'employee perspective' that prioritizes justice, fairness, autonomy and equality. This incorporates theories that do not fit the 'toolkit' approach, but which provide genuine insights into management and organization. Marxist analyses, Foucault's theorizing about surveillance and the self, Whyte's concern about groupthink and the crushing of individuality, and gender perspectives on leadership are a few such theories we have discussed in this book. This additional perspective provides students with a richer management education than the standard managerial lens.

With regard to ideology, the most influential management textbooks encourage students to see the field in ways that are consistent with a free market, manager-knows-best way, a political position that is largely hidden behind a façade of science and objectivity.

This narrow view does students a disservice. It results in original theories, like Lewin's thinking on change or Follett's on group dynamics, being twisted in ways that their authors did not intend. But beyond that, it is problematic in sending a message to students that being a manager means supporting free-market capitalism (despite some of the earliest management theories, like scientific management, emerging as a response to rampant capitalism). We do not believe that socializing students into a singular ideological position is what a university education should be about.

The present: Creating new management theory

We have been critical of the conventional view of management theory. However, critique has limited value unless it can free us from unquestioned assumptions and enable us to think differently (to paraphrase Michel Foucault). Critical thinking, therefore, can be the path to creativity and innovation. That even the most familiar theoretical foundation stones of management can be questioned and seen differently, as we have sought to show here, indicates that management in the present can still be developed and made anew. If management's history is malleable, then its future must be too.

It is reassuring that across multiple disciplines, there is growing interest in re-examining established theories. In psychology and medicine, this renewed interest is taking the form of a 'replication crisis', in which scholars are finding it difficult to reproduce the findings of classic studies, raising concerns about their validity. In management studies, critical historical research and its implications for how the field is taught to students is flourishing, with recent special issues in two leading journals, *Academy of Management Learning & Education* and *Management Learning*.

Our contribution to this literature has been re-examining the 'classic' theories of management. But our research has a major limitation. While we promote new ways of thinking about Taylor, Smith and others, we are reinforcing the same old historical figures. They were not a diverse group, being almost exclusively white, male and Anglo-American. Subsequent theoretical developments in management have been similarly pale, stale and male. The links that Mary Parker Follett established between diversity and creativity a century ago remain to be fully explored and utilized in management theorizing.

To revitalize management theory and especially our textbooks, we need, therefore, to consider and incorporate voices that have been excluded or not properly heard. Rising to meet this need is a new breed of management theorists, exploring how management theory might be different if we incorporated the views of indigenous peoples, and precolonial peoples, and minority populations, and more gender-diverse perspectives. Two cases in point are the work of Stella Nkomo, and Leon Prieto and Simone Phipps.

Nkomo (2011) examined the representation of 'African' management in textbooks. She found that apart from the ubiquitous mention of the building of Egyptian pyramids, it is largely invisible. The Egyptian case is itself problematic because in the typical narrative it is a precursor to management theory – an idea developed before (and therefore inferior to) the development of formal management theory, beginning with scientific management.

Prieto and Phipps (2019) came to a similar conclusion, pointing out that few textbooks mention Charles Clinton Spaulding, 'the father of African American management'. Spaulding's management style stemmed from his Christian faith and spirituality. He saw himself as an instrument of God, which gave him humility, a sense of mission and a commitment to co-operation.

Spaulding's (1927a, 1927b) article 'The administration of big business' outlined eight fundamentals of management. Most important was co-operation and teamwork. This was 11 years before Chester Barnard's (1938) classic *Functions of the Executive*. It was 22 years before Henri Fayol's classic *General and Industrial Management* (1916/1949), which contained 14 principles of management, was translated into English from French. Both Barnard and Fayol are regular features of management textbooks. These textbooks could have chosen Spaulding as the pre-eminent theorist of principles of general management, but they did not.

To address this deficit of African management theory, Prieto and Phipps make a convincing case for why management students should be taught the theory of co-operative advantage, a counter to the well-known theory of competitive advantage developed by Michael Porter (1985). Porter argued that firms could gain a competitive advantage through producing goods cheaper than their competitors, producing goods that were different from their competitors, and focusing on niche markets. His theory has had enormous influence but is criticized for portraying humans as rational, self-interested and individualistic.

Prieto and Phipps' (2019) theory of co-operative advantage, in contrast, assumes humans are social, communal and co-operative rather than just competitive. It draws on the African tradition of Ubuntu, which is based on spirituality, consensus building and dialogue. Spirituality can be developed by creating meaningful work, a sense of community and a genuinely caring organization. Consensus building involves allowing employees to self-organize their work arrangements where possible and ensuring that they have a voice and feel included. Leaders seek consensus, but only after all stakeholders have had a chance to contribute to the discussion.

Thankfully, there are many other scholars like Nkomo, Prieto and Phipps who are looking back in time or transgressing other assumed boundaries to draw lessons from the past that contribute to new theories of management for today and into the future.

The future: Will new theories of management enter the mainstream?

We have made the point throughout this book that textbooks play a powerful role in constructing what we take 'management' to be. The idea that academic fields are socially constructed means that while some foundations, such as Frederick Taylor and scientific management, are considered by mainstream management textbooks to be 'set in stone', they can, in fact, be shifted.

Acknowledging this is not to underestimate the challenge of achieving a shift. Best-selling textbooks have been through multiple editions because they have been successful. Success can breed a reluctance to change. Will Louis Brandeis be acknowledged for the role he played in popularizing scientific management? Will Maslow's pyramid be removed because Maslow didn't create it and because it's a poor representation of his theory? Will change management theorists look again at the assumption that their field is underpinned by Kurt Lewin's classic unfreeze–change–refreeze theory?

It is pleasing to see some textbooks are shifting their representation of Lewin and Maslow in response to this kind of questioning. But there are more significant and controversial issues to be addressed, such as the role of slavery in the history of management.

As histories from fields other than management have noted, slavery could be regarded as the birthplace of American capitalism (Desmond, 2019). And yet, as Cooke (2003) and Rosenthal (2018) have pointed out, slavery is excluded from histories of management. Prior to the so-called emergence of 'modern management', 4 million slaves were being managed in the United States. Cooke shows how scientific management, generally attributed to Taylor half a century later, was a feature of the plantations through the separation of the conception of the work from its execution. Also in use were classic management concepts such as the division of labour and the chain of command.

In 2003, Cooke accused the field of management of being in denial, since it has 'not exhibited even superficial curiosity about how these four million enslaved people were managed, at the very time and in the very nation where it claims management to have been born' (2003: 1898). Not much has changed since Cooke wrote those words. His call for the field of management to acknowledge racism against African-Americans as a contributing factor in its historical development remains a pressing concern, especially in the wake of the killing of George Floyd by a Minneapolis police officer in 2020.

There are also difficult issues to address for those who are creating alternative theories of management. For example, Nkomo identifies three tensions in writing about African management knowledge for inclusion in a body of knowledge where Western values are dominant. First, because of the prevailing managerial perspective, it is tempting to demonstrate how African ideas can be adopted to make organizations more profitable, which loses sight of their original intent. Second, 'African management' is often portrayed as a homogeneous concept, suggesting that all people in this large and diverse continent share the same beliefs and values. Sweeping generalizations can be made that ignore important differences among Africans and their approach to management. Finally, there is a tendency, in looking back to what Africa was like before it was colonized, to present African culture as 'stuck in time' – a static, historical relic rather than as something dynamic and shifting over time.

Similar difficulties face others who seek to think about management theory differently. But the pioneering work of Nkomo and others shows that it can be done. It is an endeavour well worth pursuing – and imperative if management is not to become trite, stuck in time and increasingly irrelevant.

Conclusion: Doing management differently

While the focus of this book has been on theory, we don't want to leave you with the impression that this has been merely an academic exercise. If we can *think* about theory differently, there is the possibility that we can *act* differently too. Returning to the quote from Chapter 1 that Kurt Lewin may never have said: 'There is nothing so practical as a good theory'. Our ultimate aim is to encourage people to *do* management differently.

Take as an example the simplistic management/leadership binary which we discussed in Chapter 5. This feeds the misconception that managers are bad and leaders are good, that organizations cannot change without heroic leaders, and because change is good and not changing is bad, heroic leaders (rather than good managers) are what we need. It promotes a view of leadership that is about creating and selling a vision to employees, rather than listening to and empathizing with them, and actually seeking to better understand the opportunities and challenges facing the organization – as Kurt Lewin advised more than 70 years ago.

We've seen many organizations damaged by 'transformational leaders' appointed from outside to implement 'their' grand vision. They generally don't understand the organization, they alienate the people who know it well, and by the time the leaders' dreams turn into other people's nightmares they're off on the next leg of their leadership journey. By *thinking* differently about the assumption that leadership trumps management, and understanding why, in the past, management researchers recognized that heroic theories of leadership had big drawbacks, we can encourage acting differently in the future.

Understanding how and why the misrepresentations that have been endemic in presenting the development of management theory have happened gives us valuable insight. It also creates a space for alternative ways of learning about management, and of practising management, to take hold. And given the pressing environmental, social and economic challenges the world faces today, it is a good time to try to think more creatively about people, organizations and how we work.

We hope you have enjoyed this journey through the evolution of management theory. We hope you find valuable the critical insights we've covered along the way (reproduced in summary in Table 7.1). We trust that they can help you be better critical thinkers, and more innovative management thinkers and practitioners.

Table 7.1   Twenty insights on management theory

1. Scientific management became popular because of concerns about the power of big business.

2. Adam Smith believed an ethical system should underpin economics and management.

3. Weber did not believe bureaucracy was the ideal organizational form.

4. Follett teaches us that organizations are unique, and we should understand the diverse perspectives within them.

(Continued)

Table 7.1   *(Continued)*

5. Human relations theories, like scientific management, emerged to address a crisis in capitalism.

6. Motivation theories were translated for a management audience, and meaning was lost in the process.

7. Marxist analyses argue low motivation is a product of employment relations within capitalism.

8. Bentham's panopticon highlights that being under surveillance can be a major source of motivation.

9. The Myers-Briggs personality test appeals to managers and employees but has no scientific credibility.

10. Theories of the self show how organizations categorize and control employees.

11. Management textbooks celebrate teamworking but have forgotten earlier concerns about the loss of individuality, creativity and critical thinking.

12. Understanding culture management as an intensification of control over employees highlights the relevance of past debates about conformity.

13. Simplistic distinctions between 'leadership' and 'management' are unhelpful.

14. Collective forms of leadership can overcome the dangers of individual-based approaches.

15. Challenging the origins of change management theory provides a more balanced view of stability and change.

16. Challenging common-sense theories of what good leadership is can inspire new thinking.

17. Milton Friedman and Edward Freeman's theories of Corporate Social Responsibility are not the opposites we are led to believe.

18. Ethical theories taken from moral philosophy provide insights, but have blind spots.

19. The 'robber barons' and their philanthropy illuminates the social responsibilities of governments and corporations.

20. The Quakers adopted a paternalistic approach well before theories about corporate culture emerged.

Search *VSFI Management Theory* in YouTube to watch videos relating to each critical insight.

Appendix: Resources for Studying Management Theory Critically

█████ Recommended reading

This book draws on research we have produced on the origins of foundational theories in management, in particular:

Pol, O., Bridgman, T., and Cummings, S. (2020) Whyte-out: How the creator of groupthink became unseen by management's history. *Proceedings of the 80th Annual Meeting of the Academy of Management*, Vancouver, 7-11 August.

Bednarek, R., Cummings, S., and Bridgman, T. (2020) Out of place: Management studies' temporal misplacements of Mary Parker Follett. *80th Academy of Management Annual Meeting*, Vancouver, 7-11 August.

Bridgman, T., Cummings, S., and Ballard, J. (2019) Who built Maslow's pyramid? A history of the creation of management studies' most famous symbol and its implications for management education. *Academy of Management Learning & Education*, 18(1): 81–98.

Badham, R., Bridgman, T., and Cummings, S. (2019) The organisation-as-iceberg metaphor: A strong defence for historical re-surfacing. *35th EGOS Colloquium*, Edinburgh, 4-6 July.

Cummings, S., Bridgman, T., Hassard, J., and Rowlinson, M. (2017) *A New History of Management*. Cambridge: Cambridge University Press.

Bridgman, T., Cummings, S., and McLaughlin, C. (2016) Re-stating the case: How revisiting the development of the case method can help us think differently about the future of the business school. *Academy of Management Learning & Education*, 15(4): 724–41.

Cummings, S. and Bridgman, T. (2016) The limits and possibilities of history: How a wider, deeper and more engaged understanding of business history can foster innovative thinking. *Academy of Management Learning & Education*, 15(2): 250–67.

Cummings, S. and Bridgman, T. (2016) How recovering Adam Smith can help us think differently about the foundations of management. *Proceedings of the 76th Annual Meeting of the Academy of Management*, Anaheim, 5–9 August.

Cummings, S., Bridgman, T., and Brown, K. (2016) Unfreezing change as three steps: Rethinking Kurt Lewin's legacy for change management. *Human Relations*, 69(1): 33–60.

Cummings, S. and Bridgman, T. (2014) The origin of management is sustainability: Recovering an alternative theoretical foundation for management. *Proceedings of the 74th Annual Meeting of the Academy of Management*, Philadelphia, 1–5 August.

Cummings, S. and Bridgman, T. (2011) The relevant past: Why the history of management should be critical for our future. *Academy of Management Learning & Education*, 10(1): 77–93.

Recommended watching

Animated videos for each of the 20 insights on management theory in Table 7.1 can be viewed at the Sage Students YouTube Channel.

In addition, animated video summaries of the research listed above are available to watch at our *A New History of Management* YouTube Channel (www.youtube.com/channel/UCVTvua598jsA0PPeGK4FnSg).

The following documentaries were mentioned in the book:

Dirty Money: Hard Nox (2018), Netflix.

On the Line (1924) *People's Century*. Public Broadcasting Service.

The Investor: Out for Blood in Silicon Valley (2019), HBO.

Trump's Road to the White House (2017) *Frontline*, Public Broadcasting Service.

Recommended listening

TALKING ABOUT
ORGANIZATIONS
PODCAST

Talking about Organizations Podcast (@talkaboutorgs) is a free, not-for-profit weekly conversational podcast on well-known theories in management. Each episode features one book, journal article or idea where the hosts discuss its purpose and impact. Topic areas include the classics, organizational theory, organizational behaviour, digital economy, human resources, methodology and human resources. Episodes are available at the website www.talkingaboutorganizations.com/ and on Spotify.

Recommended doing

Who killed Adam Smith? Figure that out for yourself in this innovative murder mystery podcast developed by Stuart Middleton, Cameron Morgan and Shakira Moss from University of Queensland. The murder mystery podcast was developed to teach university students management history from a critical perspective. https://teach.business.uq.edu.au/articulate/case-of-invisible-hand

References

Abrahamson, E. (2004) Avoiding repetitive change syndrome. *MIT Sloan Management Review*, Winter: 93–5.

Acker, J. and Van Houten, D.R. (1974) Differential recruitment and control: The sex structuring of organizations. *Administrative Science Quarterly*, 19(2): 152–63.

Adams, J.S. (1965) Inequity in social exchanges. In L. Berkowitz (ed.), *Advances in Experimental Social Psychology*. Volume 2. New York: Academic Press, pp. 267–300.

Alderfer, C.P. (1969) An empirical test of a new theory of human needs. *Organizational Behavior and Human Performance*, 4: 142–75.

Alderfer, C.P. (1989) Theories reflecting my personal experience and life development. *Journal of Applied Behavioral Science*, 25(4): 351–65.

Alvesson, M. and Sandberg, J. (2012) Has management studies lost its way? Ideas for more imaginative and innovative research. *Journal of Management Studies*, 50(1): 128–52.

Asch, S.E. (1958) Effects of group pressure upon modification and distortion of judgments. In E.E Maccoby, T.M. Newcomb and E.L. Hartley (eds.), *Readings in Social Psychology*. 3rd edn. New York: Holt, Rinehart and Winston, pp. 174–83.

Avolio, B.J. and Gardner, W.L. (2005) Authentic leadership development: Getting to the root of positive forms of leadership. *The Leadership Quarterly*, 16: 315–38.

Barnard, C.I. (1938) *The Functions of the Executive*. Cambridge, MA: Harvard University Press.

Barrett, L.F. (2017) The secret history of emotions. *The Chronicle of Higher Education*, March 5 (www.chronicle.com/article/The-Secret-History-of-Emotions/239357?fbclid=IwAR03i8XQeZnPgspwq1Yg vB4rT-IK-8K0iCMBCjUhAmZqcwjq-6zTvBn76mg#comments-anchor)

Bass, B.M. and Riggio, R.E. (2006) *Transformational Leadership*. 2nd edn. Mahwah, NJ: Lawrence Erlbaum Associates.

Bauman, Z. (1989) *Modernity and the Holocaust*. Oxford: Polity Press.

Bell, E., Panayiotou, A., and Sayers, J. (2019) Reading the TED talk genre: Contradictions and pedagogical pleasures in spreading ideas about management. *Academy of Management Learning & Education* (journals.aom.org/doi/10.5465/amle.2017.0323).

Billig, M. (2014) Kurt Lewin's leadership studies and his legacy to social psychology: Is there nothing as practical as a good theory? *Journal for the Theory of Social Behaviour*, 45(4): 440–60.

Brandeis, L.D. (1911) *Scientific Management and the Railroads*. New York: Engineering Magazine.

Braverman, H. (1974) *Labor and Monopoly Capital*. New York: Monthly Review Press.

Burns, J.M. (1978) *Leadership*. New York: Harper and Row.

Cameron, K.S., Ireland, R.D., Lussier, R.N., New, J.R., and Robbins, S.P. (2003) Management textbooks as propaganda. *Journal of Management Education*, 27(6): 711–29.

Carroll, A.B. (1991) The pyramid of corporate social responsibility: Toward the moral management of organizational stakeholders. *Business Horizons*, July–August: 39–48.

Carroll, B., Firth, J., Ford, J., and Taylor, S. (2018) The social construction of leadership studies: Representations of rigour and relevance in textbooks. *Leadership*, 14(2): 159–78.

Chandler, A.D. (1962) *Strategy and Structure: Chapters in the History of the American Industrial Enterprise*. Cambridge, MA: Harvard University Press.

Clegg, S.R., Kornberger, M., Pitsis, T.S., and Mount, M. (2019) *Managing and Organizations: An Introduction to Theory and Practice*. 5th edn. Los Angeles, CA: Sage.

Cooke, B. (2003) The denial of slavery in management studies. *Journal of Management Studies*, 40(8): 1895–918.

Cooke, B. and Mills, A.J. (2008) The right to be human and human rights: Maslow, McCarthyism and the death of humanist theories of management. *Management & Organizational History*, 3(1): 27–47.

Copley, F.B. (1923) *Frederick W. Taylor: Father of Scientific Management*. Volume 2. New York: Harper and Brothers.

Davis, K. (1957) *Human Relations in Business*. New York: McGraw-Hill.

Dellheim, C. (1987) The creation of a company culture: Cadburys, 1861–1931. *The American Historical Review*, 92: 13–44.

Desmond, M. (2019) In order to understand the brutality of American capitalism, you have to start on the plantation. *New York Times*, August 14 (www.nytimes.com/interactive/2019/08/14/magazine/slavery-capitalism.html).

Donham, W.B. (1932) *Business Looks at the Unforseen*. New York: Whittlesey House/McGraw-Hill.

Drezner, D.W. (2017) *The Ideas Industry*. New York: Oxford University Press.

Drucker, P.F. (1995) Introduction: Mary Parker Follett: Prophet of Management. In P. Graham (ed.), *Mary Parker Follett Prophet of Management*. Boston, MA: Harvard Business School Press, pp. 1–9.

Earley, P.C. (1989) Social loafing and collectivism: A comparison of the United States and the People's Republic of China. *Administrative Science Quarterly*, 34(4): 565–81.

Empson, L. (2018) If you're so successful, why are you still working 70 hours a week? *Harvard Business Review*, February (hbr.org/2018/02/if-youre-so-successful-why-are-you-still-working-70-hours-a-week).

Emre, M. (2019) *The Personality Brokers: The Strange History of Myers-Briggs and the Birth of Personality Testing*. London: Penguin/Random House.

Fayol, H. (1916) Administration industrielle et générale-Prévoyance. *Organization, Commandement, Coordination, Contrôle*. Paris: H. Dunod et E. Pinat.

Fayol, H. (1949) *General and Industrial Management*. London: Pitman.

Fiedler, F.E. (1967) *A Theory of Leadership Effectiveness*. New York: McGraw-Hill.

Follett, M.P. (1918) *The New State*: London: Longmans, Green and Company.

Follett, M. P. (1924) *Creative Experience*. New York: Longmans, Green and Company.

Follett, M.P. (1925) Constructive conflict. In P. Graham (ed.) (1995) *Mary Parker Follett: Prophet of Management*. Boston, MA: Harvard Business School Press.

Foucault, M. (1979) *Discipline and Punish: The Birth of the Prison*. London: Allen Lane.

Foucault, M. (1985) *The History of Sexuality: Volume Two: The Use of Pleasure*. New York: Pantheon.

Fox, A. (1966) Managerial ideology and labour relations. *British Journal of Industrial Relations*, 4(1–3): 366–78.

Freeman, R.E. (1984) *Strategic Management: A Stakeholder Approach*. Boston, MA: Pitman.

Freeman, R.E., Harrison, J.S., Wicks, A.C., Parmar, B.L., and de Colle, S. (2010) *Stakeholder Theory: The State of the Art*. Cambridge: Cambridge University Press.

French, W.L. and Bell, C.H. (1995) *Organization Development*. 5th edn. Englewood Cliffs, NJ: Prentice-Hall.

Friedman, M. (1962) *Capitalism and Freedom*. Chicago, IL: University of Chicago Press.

Friedman, M. (1970) The social responsibility of business is to increase its profits. *The New York Times* magazine, September 13.

George, C.S. (1968/1972) *The History of Management Thought*. Englewood Cliffs, NJ: Prentice-Hall.

Gilbreth, F.B. and Carey, E.G. (1948) *Cheaper by the Dozen*. New York: Thomas Y. Crowell.

Gillard, J. (2014) *My Story*. Sydney, NSW: Random House.

Goffman, E. (1959) *The Presentation of Self in Everyday Life*. New York: Doubleday.

Gordon, R. (2016) *The Rise and Fall of American Growth: The US Standard of Living Since the Civil War*. Princeton, NJ: Princeton University Press.

Gordon, R. and Howell, J. (1959) *Higher Education for Business*. New York: Columbia University Press.

Grant, A. (2013) Goodbye to the MBTI, the fad that won't die. *Psychology Today*, September 18 (www.psychologytoday.com/nz/blog/give-and-take/201309/goodbye-mbti-the-fad-won-t-die).

Grant, A. (2016) Unless you're Oprah, 'be yourself' is terrible advice. *The New York Times*, June 4 (www.nytimes.com/2016/06/05/opinion/sunday/unless-youre-oprah-be-yourself-is-terrible-advice.html).

Grey, C. (2005) *A Very Short, Fairly Interesting and Reasonably Cheap Book about Studying Organizations*. London: Sage.

The Harvard Crimson (1932) Dean Donham's speech, September 21.

Hassard, J. (2012) Rethinking the Hawthorne Studies: The Western Electric Research in its social, political and historical context. *Human Relations*, 65(11): 1431–61.

Heckscher, C. (1994) Defining the post-bureaucratic type. In C. Heckscher and A. Donnellon (eds.), *The Post-bureaucratic Organization: New Perspectives on Organizational Change*. Thousand Oaks, CA: Sage, pp. 14–62.

Herzberg, F. (1968) One more time: How do you motivate employees? *Harvard Business Review*, 81(1): 87–96.

Hood, F.C. (1924, 11 January) Letter to W.B. Donham. Box 13, Folder 13–11. *Office of the Dean (Donham) Records, (AA1.1)*. Harvard Business School Archives, Baker Library, Harvard Business School.

Huczynski, A. (2006) *Management Gurus*. Revised edn. London: Routledge.

Irfan, U. (2019) UN Climate Change Report: Four ways to be smarter about land use to fight climate chane, *Vox*, August 9 (www.vox.com/science-and-health/2019/8/9/20791617/climate-report-2019-un-land-ipcc-solutions).

Jackson, B. and Parry, K. (2018) *A Very Short, Fairly Interesting and Reasonably Cheap Book about Studying Leadership*. 3rd edn. London: Sage.

Jacques, R.S. (2006) History, historiography and organization studies: The challenge and the potential. *Management and Organizational History*, 1(1): 31–49.

Janis, I.L. (1971) Groupthink. *Psychology Today*, 26: 43–6, 74–6.

Janis, I.L. (1972) *Victims of Groupthink: A Psychological Study of Foreign-policy Secisions and Fiascoes*. Boston, MA: Houghton, Mifflin.

Jenkins, K. (2003) *Refiguring History: New Thoughts on an Old Discipline*. London: Routledge.

Jung, C.G. (1923) *Psychological Types*. London: Kegan Paul.

Karau, S.J. and Williams, K.D. (1993) Social loafing: A meta-analytic review and theoretical integration. *Interpersonal Relations and Group Processes*, 65(4): 681–706.

Kaufman, S.B. (2019) *Authenticity under fire*. June 14 (blogs.scientificamerican.com/beautiful-minds/authenticity-under-fire/).

Kavanagh, D. and Brigham, M. (2018) The Quakers: Forgotten pioneers. In T. Peltonen, H. Gaggiotti and P. Case (eds.), *Origins of Organizing*. Cheltenham, UK: Edward Elgar, pp. 147–66.

Khurana, R. (2007) *From Higher Aims to Hired Hands*. Princeton, NJ: Princeton University Press.

Klein, N. (2017) *This Changes Everything: Capitalism vs. the Climate*. London: Penguin Books.

Koontz, H. and O'Donnell, C. (1955) *Principles of Management: An Analysis of Managerial Functions*. New York: McGraw-Hill.

Kotter, J.P. (1995) Leading change: Why transformation efforts fail. *Harvard Business Review*, March/April: 59–67.

Kotter, J.P. (1996 and 2012) *Leading Change*. Boston, MA: Harvard Business School Press.

Kotter, J.P. and Schlesinger, L.A. (1979) Choosing strategies for change. *Harvard Business Review*, 57(2), March–April: 106–14. Reprinted in 2008.

Learmonth, M. and Morrell, K. (2019) *Critical Perspectives on Leadership: The Language of Corporate Power*. New York: Routledge.

Lewin, K. (1947) Frontiers in group dynamics: Concept, method and reality in social science; equilibrium and social change. *Human Relations*, 1(1): 5–41.

Lewin, K. (1951) *Field Theory in Social Science: Selected Theoretical Papers*. Ed. D. Cartwright. New York: Harper and Row.

Lussier, K. (2019) Of Maslow, motives, and managers: The hierarchy of needs in American business, 1960–1985. *Journal of the History of the Behavioral Sciences*. (onlinelibrary.wiley.com/doi/abs/10.1002/jhbs.21992).

Marens, R. (2012) Generous in victory? American managerial autonomy, labour relations and the invention of Corporate Social Responsibility. *Socio-Economic Review*, 10: 59–84.

Maslow, A.H. (1943) A theory of human motivation. *Psychological Review*, 50(4): 370–96.

Maslow, A.H. (1954, 1970, 1987) *Motivation and Personality*. New York: Harper and Row.

Matthews, D. (2018) The case against billionaire philanthropy. *Vox*, December 17 (www.vox.com/future-perfect/2018/12/17/18141181/foundation-charity-deduction-democracy-rob-reich).

Mayer, J.P. (1943) *Max Weber and German Politics*. London: Faber and Faber.

Mayo, E. (1933) *The Human Problems of an Industrial Civilization*. New York: Macmillan.

McDermid, C.D. (1960) How money motivates men. *Business Horizons*, 3(4): 93–100.

McFarland, D.E. (1958) *Management: Principles and Practices*. New York: Macmillan.

McGregor, D.M. (1960) *The Human Side of Enterprise*. New York: McGraw-Hill.

Mead, G.H. (1934) *Mind, Self and Society*. Chicago, IL: University of Chicago Press.

Metcalf, H.C. and Urwick, L. (1940/2004) *Dynamic Administration: The Collected Papers of Mary Parker Follett*. 1st edn. New York: Routledge.

Milgram, S. (1974) *Obedience to Authority: An Experimental View*. New York: Harper and Row.

Muhr, S.L. and Sullivan, K.R. (2013) 'None so queer as folk': Gendered expectations and transgressive bodies in leadership. *Leadership*, 9(3): 416–35.

Nelson, D.L. and Quick, J.C. (2013) *Organizational Behavior: Science, the Real World and You*. 8th edn. Mason, OH: Cengage Learning.

Nkomo, S.M. (2011) A postcolonial and anti-colonial reading of 'African' leadership and management in organization studies: Tensions, contradictions and possibilities. *Organization*, 18(3): 365–86.

O'Connor, E.S. (1999) The politics of management thought: A case study of the Harvard Business School and the Human Relations School. *Academy of Management Review*, 24(1): 117–31.

O'Doherty, D. and Vachhani, S. (2017) Individual differences, personality and self. In D. Knights and H. Willmott (eds.), *Introducing Organizational Behaviour and Management*. Andover, UK: Cengage Learning, pp. 78–112.

Orwell, G. (1949). *Nineteen Eighty-four*. London: Secker & Warburg.

Ouchi, W.G. (1981) *Theory Z: How American Business Can Meet the Japanese Challenge*. Reading, MA: Addison-Wesley.

Parker, M. (2002) *Against Management: Organization in the Age of Managerialism*. Cambridge, UK: Polity Press.

Pascale, R.T. and Athos, A.G. (1981) *The Art of Japanese Management*. Harmondsworth: Penguin.

Peters, T. and Waterman, R. (1982) *In Search of Excellence: Lessons from America's Best Run Companies*. London and New York: Harper Row.

Pfeffer, J. (2015) *Leadership BS: Fixing Workplaces and Careers One Truth at a Time*. New York: Harper Business.

Pierson, F. (1959) *The Education of American Businessmen: A Study of University-Collegiate Programs in Business Education*. New York: McGraw-Hill.

Porter, M.E. (1985) *The Competitive Advantage: Creating and Sustaining Superior Performance*. New York: Free Press.

Prieto, L.C. and Phipps, T.A. (2019) *African American Management History*. Bingley, UK: Emerald.

Reich, R. (2018) *Just Giving: Why Philanthropy is Failing Democracy and How it Can Do Better*. Princeton, NJ: Princeton University Press.

Reichers, A., Wanous, J., and Austin, J. (1997) Understanding and managing cynicism about organizational change. *Academy of Management Executive*, 11(1): 48–59.

Ringelmann, M. (1913) Recherches sur les moteurs animes: Travail de l'homme [Research on animate sources of power: The work of man]. *Annales de l'Institut National Agronomique*, 2e serie-tome XII, 1–40.

Robbins, S.P., DeCenzo, D., Coulter, M., and Woods, M. (2016) *Management: The Essentials*. 3rd edn. Melbourne, Vic.: Pearson.

Roberts, J. (2017) Motivation and the self. In D. Knights and H. Willmott (eds.), *Introducing Organizational Behaviour and Management*. Andover, UK: Cengage Learning, pp. 40–77.

Rosenthal, C. (2018) *Accounting for Slavery: Masters and Management*. Cambridge, MA: Harvard University Press.

Samson, D., Donnet, T., and Daft, R.L. (2018) *Management*. Melbourne, Vic.: Cengage.

Schein, E.H. (2010) *Organizational Culture and Leadership*. San Francisco, CA: Jossey Bass.

Schein, E.H. (2015a) Organizational psychology then and now: Some observations. *Annual Review of Organizational Psychology and Organizational Behavior*, 2: 1–19.

Schein, E.H. (2015b) *Destroy the iceberg (Reported discussion of iceberg metaphor)*, Brighton Leadership Group, October 6 (bright onleadership.com/2015/10/06/destroy-the-iceberg/).

Schermerhorn, J.R., Davidson, P., Woods, P., Factor, A., Simon, A., McBarron, E., and Janaid, F. (2020) *Management*. 7th Asia-Pacific edn. Milton, Qld: Wiley.

Schubert, J.N., Stewart, P.A., and Curran, M.A. (2002) A defining presidential moment: 9/11 and the rally effect. *Political Psychology*, 23(3): 559–83.

Sinclair, A. (2005) *Doing Leadership Differently*. 2nd edn. Melbourne, Vic.: Melbourne University Press.

Sinclair, A. (2007) *Leadership for the Disillusioned: Moving Beyond Myths and Heroes to Leading that Liberates*. London: Allen and Unwin.

Smith, A. (1759/2010) *The Theory of Moral Sentiments* (with an Introduction by A. Sen). Harmondsworth: Penguin Classics.

Smith, A. (1776/2012) *The Wealth of Nations*. Ware, UK: Wordsworth Editions Ltd.

Smith, A., Tennent, K., and Russell, J.D. (2019) The rejection of industrial democracy by Berle and Means and the emergence of the ideology of managerialism. *Economic and Industrial Democracy*, October 30 (journals.sagepub.com/doi/full/10.1177/0143831X 19883683).

Spaulding, C.C. (1927a) The administration of big business. *The Pittsburgh Courier*, August 13, p. 4.

Spaulding, C.C. (1927b) The administration of big business. *The Pittsburgh Courier*, August 20, p. 8.

Stogdill, R.M. (1948) Personal factors associated with leadership: A survey of the literature. *Journal of Psychology*, 25(1): 35–71.

Stoner, J. (1982) *Management*. Englewood Cliffs, NJ: Prentice-Hall.

Tarbell, I. (1904) *The History of the Standard Oil Company*. New York: McClur Phillips & Co.

Taylor, F.W. (1903) *Shop Management*. New York: Harper and Row.

Taylor, F.W. (1911) *The Principles of Scientific Management*. New York: Harper and Row.

Taylor, S. (2015) Trait theories on leaders and leadership: From Ancient Greece to twenty-first-century neuroscience. In B. Carroll, J. Ford and S. Taylor (eds.), *Leadership: Contemporary Critical Perspectives*. Thousand Oaks, CA: Sage, pp. 26–44.

Terry, G. R. (1956) *Principles of Management*. Homewood, IL: Richard D. Irwin Inc.

The Book of Life. The importance of Maslow's pyramid of needs. Available at: www.theschooloflife.com/thebookoflife/the-importance-of-maslows-pyramid-of-needs/.

TIME. (2014) *The 25 most influential business management books.* Available at: content.time.com/time/specials/packages/completelist/ 0,29569,2086680,00.html (accessed 3 March, 2020).

Tonn, J.C. (2003) *Mary P. Follett: Creating Democracy, Transforming Management.* New Haven, CT: Yale University Press.

Tourish, D. (2013) *The Dark Side of Transformational Leadership: A Critical Perspective.* London: Routledge, pp. 20–39.

Tuckman, B. (1965) Developmental sequence in small groups. *Psychological Bulletin,* 63(6): 384–99.

Tuckman, B. and Jensen, M.C. (1977) Stages of small-group development revisited. *Group and Organization Studies,* 2(4): 419–27.

Veblen, T. (1918) *The Higher Learning in America: A Memorandum on the Conduct of Universities by Businessmen.* New York: B.W. Huebsch.

Vroom, V.H. (1964) *Work and Motivation.* New York: Wiley.

Wahba, M.A. and Bridwell, L.G. (1976) Maslow reconsidered: A review of research on the need hierarchy theory. *Organizational Behavior and Human Performance,* 15: 212–40.

Walker, B.W. and Caprar, D.V. (2019) When performance gets personal: Towards a theory of performance-based identity. *Human Relations,* June 20 (doi.org/10.1177/0018726719851835).

Walsh, J.P. (2005) Book review essay: Taking stock of stakeholder management. *Academy of Management Review,* 30(2): 426–52.

Weber, M. (1948) *From Max Weber: Essays in Sociology.* Translated by H. Gerth and C.W. Mills. London: Routledge.

Whitehead, A.N. (1925) *Science and the Modern World.* New York: Macmillan.

Whyte, W.H. (1952) Groupthink. *Fortune,* March.

Whyte, W.H. (1956) *The Organization Man.* New York: Simon and Schuster.

Willmott, H. (1993) Strength is ignorance; Slavery is freedom: Managing culture in modern organizations. *Journal of Management Studies,* 30(4): 515–52.

Wray-Bliss, E. (2017) Ethics at work. In D. Knights and H. Willmott (eds.), *Introducing Organizational Behaviour and Management.* Andover, UK: Cengage Learning, pp. 564–95.

Wren, D.A. (1972) *The Evolution of Management Thought.* New York: The Ronald Press.

Wren, D.A. (1994) *The Evolution of Management Thought.* 4th edn. New York: Wiley.

Zaleznik, A. (1977) Managers and leaders: Are they different? *Harvard Business Review,* May–June.

Index

Page numbers in **bold** indicate tables and in *italic* indicate figures.